All About
Attention Deficit Disorder

Symptoms, Diagnosis and Treatment:
Children and Adults

All About Attention Deficit Disorder

Thomas W. Phelan, Ph.D.

CHILD MANAGEMENT INC
Glen Ellyn, Illinois

Cover design and illustrations by Margaret Mayer
Cover photography by Steve Orlick
Child Management Logo by Steve Roe

Printed in the United States of America
10 9 8 7 6 5 4 3 2 1

For more information, contact:
Child Management, Inc.
800 Roosevelt Road
Glen Ellyn, Illinois 60137

Publisher's Cataloging in Publication
(Prepared by Quality Books Inc.)
Phelan, Thomas W., 1943-
    All about attention deficit disorder / Thomas W. Phelan.
    p. cm.
    Includes bibliographical references.

    1. Attention-deficit hyperactivity disorder--Popular works. 2. Hyperactive children.   I. Title.

RJ506.H9P44 1996   618.92'8589
                          QBI96-40336

To the people of our ADD support groups:

Never has so much
Been done for so many
By so few...
So fast

Contents

i

Part II: Diagnosing Attention Deficit

Part III: Multimodal Treatment of ADD

Part IV: ADD in Adults

Introduction

A ttention Deficit Disorder (ADD or ADHD) is getting more and more attention itself these days. Not too long ago, some of this had to do with the controversy surrounding medication treatment. More recently and more positively, ADD received a good deal of recognition during the successful struggle to get it recognized as a handicapping condition under Federal special education law.

ADD should get a lot of attention. It affects a tremendous number of children *and adults*, and it is a pervasive, serious, noncurable condition. Estimates of the incidence of Attention Deficit Disorder generally range around five percent of the school age population and around three percent of the adult population. This means, on the average, about one ADD child per classroom, but the true impact of the ADD problem is made more graphic when you consider that in any school system it is likely that 40% of the problem children are likely to be Attention Deficit Disorder kids.

ADD might be described as a concentration problem with a personality to go along with it—kind of like a "space cadet with an attitude." ADD people have a terrible time focusing on things they

1

don't like, such as schoolwork, and their temperaments are most often—but not always—the intense, restless, "wired" variety. They therefore present a tremendous problem both to themselves as well as to those who have to deal with them.

Fortunately, Attention Deficit Disorder has been the focus of a lot of research in the last 20 years. There is now a lot of useful information available. Unfortunately, this information is still slowly and erratically filtering down to those who need it: parents, teachers, principals, pediatricians, psychologists, and the ADD children and adults themselves. In some places, ignorance and myths about ADD still abound; in other places, fortunate families find state of the art practice to help them along their way.

The available information about ADD has also changed some recently. ADD—or what used to be called hyperactivity or hyperkinesis, for example, used to be associated with brain damage. Later, researchers discovered this was usually not the case. It also used to be thought that the vast majority of ADD kids were boys. Some people now think that the sex ratio might be about equal. The name for "whatever it is" has similarly changed. "Minimal Brain Dysfunction" gave way to "Hyperkinetic Reaction of Childhood." Then, in the research of the 1970s, there was more of a focus on the concentrational difficulties that "hyperkinetic" children experienced, and in 1980 the problem was renamed Attention Deficit Disorder.

Three types were described: ADD with hyperactivity, ADD without hyperactivity, and ADD—Residual type, referring to an adolescent or adult who had outgrown some of the gross-motor hyperactivity, but not all of the other ADD symptoms. These types are still useful categories and they will be referred to in this book. In 1987, however, the label was again altered to the rather odd ADHD, or Attention-Deficit Hyperactivity Disorder, which many people in the field consider to be an awkward and unnecessary change.

Whatever you call it, Attention Deficit Disorder is a common and usually chronic problem that has been around for a long time. It still causes a lot of trouble for a lot of children and adults.

Part I:

What Is
Attention Deficit Disorder?

1

Impact

Mom

It's April and time for the annual IEP staffing at school again about daughter, Tracy. Tom says he can't go because of an important meeting at work, so Jane is going—again—by herself. She hates these things. She sits with several teachers, a psychologist, the principal, social worker, and LD resource teacher and listens to all the things Tracy is doing wrong. She talks out in class, doesn't finish her work, doesn't pay attention, is sometimes sassy, argues or jabbers with other kids during class, etc., etc., etc.

The list every year is always the same. Then come the gentle hints about family counseling (they've already seen two counselors), setting firmer limits at home, working with Tracy more on her reading. Is the marriage OK? Is anyone depressed? What else might be going on? Finally, Jane signs the IEP forms with relief, knowing the ordeal is almost over. She hardly cares what they say at this point. Glancing at the clock, she sees it's already 4:15. The kids can get their own supper tonight—is it too early for a drink with Thelma?

Dad

The road stretches out endlessly through the rolling farm country. Des Moines is still 85 miles away and John doesn't think his sanity will last that long. The kids are warming up for another fight in the back seat. Seven year old Jeff, who's always been a difficult child, is about to provoke four year old Mary for the 4896th time during the trip. Ten minutes ago John almost lost control of the car while reaching around trying to hit Jeff. The all too predictable fight starts. Mary is screaming, crying; it looks like there's a spot of blood on her cheek.

That's it! John screeches the car off to the side. His startled wife yells at him for his carelessness. He doesn't care: right now he just wants to kill this kid. He jumps out and jerks open the back door. Jeff is now quiet and terrified by the insane look in his father's eyes. Mom is yelling, "John, for pete's sake, please, don't!" Jeff is yanked from the car, hitting his head on the door on the way out. He starts crying. Cars and trucks speed by. John drags the little monster down the grassy hill and starts spanking him as hard as he can, screaming at the top of his lungs how sick and tired he is of this @#$% and how it's going to stop once and for all and about orphanages, etc.

There is a sudden screech behind them as a car pulls up. An angry man jumps out, yelling, "What the h—l do you think you're doing to that kid!" The Good Samaritan. John tells the newcomer where to put his good intentions. Back in the car Mom and Mary are sobbing.

The Happy Couple

Marc and Susan nervously enter the restaurant with four year old Steve. Steve is cute, curious, talkative, and charming to the pleasant and attentive young waitress. His parents start relaxing a little and thinking, "Maybe this time things will be OK." But they still order, as usual, food that can be prepared very quickly. Steve wants the hot dog, but the restaurant only has the jumbo size. Susan knows he can't eat all that and she suggests the hamburger. Steve blows. He screams "HOT DOG!" six times at the top of his lungs, pulls his place mat off the table, spilling the water and sending the silverware clattering to the floor. Other people look over with the critical gazes so familiar to these parents. The looks say, "What's the matter with you?", "Why can't you control that brat?", "Why don't you eat somewhere else?" Saying nothing, Marc grabs Steve roughly and leaves for the car. Susan sits there—no longer hungry—trying to decide whether to cancel the order.

The Lucky Teacher

It's 90 degrees, mid-May, and only 2:45. School doesn't get out until 3:15. Mrs. Simpson will have to call Tommy's parents again today because he hasn't completed hardly any of his work. He has remained off task almost all day, and the fact that the air conditioning wasn't working made matters considerably worse: all the other children have been more restless and Tommy had to watch every movement each of them made.

An impossible task, but he tried. He did not try to do his math or language arts, however. For the umpteenth time this year he just couldn't work in his small study group without bothering everyone else, so she again had to move his desk. The psychologist told her to put him up front by himself, but then he is isolated—the only one in the room not in a foursome. What good does that do for his self-esteem?

Mrs. Simpson had thought 4th graders were supposed to be easier to deal with. She tried all of the things she thought might work: talking to Tommy alone, more positive reinforcement, daily sheets, parent conferences. Some things work for a while—a few days, but then...

The principal, Mr. Stock, is always pushing her to call the parents. What good is that going to do? Besides, their attitude at the last staffing was positively hostile, and Mrs. Simpson felt like she was being blamed for Tommy's attitude, his underachievement, and for all his misbehavior. The child is real nice one-on-one, but in class he's a total monster. Mrs. Simpson feels sorry for the fifth grade teacher that gets Tommy next year. But then again, he won't be retained and she'll get a break.

Or will she? Tommy has a younger brother in third grade who's starting to pull the same things his older brother does. What's wrong with that family!? Maybe selling insurance would be easier...

The Main Man

School is so boring! The main crop in Brazil is....? Man, geography is awesome! The main crop in Brazil has got to be jelly beans. That's it! No, it's probably seaweed. Who could possibly care what the main idiot crop of stupid Brazil is?

Whoa! Wait—hold the phone! There are two people in the world who could care about this earth-shaking question: my teacher, Mrs. Crippen (I prefer "Krypton") and my Perfect Older Sister who gets straight A's and always does everything right and who always needles me when my parents aren't looking. I hate her. Wait til she finds what I put in her bed before school this morning—that'll set her straight! Then, of course, she'll tell and Mom will cry and have a cow and tell Dad when he gets home and he'll probably knock me around again even before his first drink. But, still... it may still be worth it.

God, it's not even lunch time yet. OK, Brazil. Crops. Think, dummy! Who invented this garbage!? Not only is this junk boring, but Krypton won't even let you move. Once she even put a string around me and my chair and told me I'd get a detention if I broke it. So, naturally, I just had to—nobody's going to pull that on me... Had to see the old man, but he's pretty cool—most of the times I've seen him, anyway.

Brazil... Wonder if I can finish this idiot work sheet before lunch, so I don't have to bring it home and sit at the kitchen table for hours with my mother nagging and Miss Perfect getting to watch TV and laughing at me.

God, I'm hungry. A sandwich will sure taste good and then recess, where the authorities actually let you move around. Amaz-

ing, they're so kind. I may just move around some right into that brat who always gets the other kids after me. Beat him up some last week, but it didn't help much. Today I'll nail him right before the bell...

This chair has a sliver in it... Oop, Crippen's looking at me. She knows I'm not paying attention to my work again like all the other good little boys and girls. "Are you with us today, Jeffery?", "Are we paying better attention to our work today, Jeffery?" If it's our work, why doesn't she do it? Better look like I'm doing something. Head down, look at paper, move hand. Oh god, where's my pencil ... Jeez I'm an idiot!

No I'm not. Once they told me I got 125 on an IQ test. Whatever I'm supposed to have 125 of sure doesn't keep me from getting D's. D stands for Dumb. Dork. Death. Dope. Dad got D's too when he was younger. So where does he get off yelling at me all the time?

Ten minutes til food. CROPS IN BRAZIL! Ten lousy minutes. I can't stand it! When I get older, I'll drive a truck. You sit up real high and you get to keep moving. It's great. I'll take my little sister with me. Sarah's not so bad, and she doesn't do so hot in school either. She doesn't get in as much trouble as me, but the teacher calls her "spacey" sometimes. One kid heard that and started calling her Spacey Sarah on the playground, so I pushed him around and made him promise to shut up. Most of the kids at this school are jerks.

That creep behind me is popping her gum again. Drives me nuts! Sounds like forty bowls of Rice Krispies right in my ear. Then she'll start gabbing to the jerk next to her, but they'll never get in trouble. They're girls. They thought it was real funny the other day when we were having a math quiz and I didn't even know it. It was their fault! If I pulled the stuff they do, Krypton would be on me faster than you can spit.

Oh my god, here she is! Those are her shoes standing next to my desk. I didn't even see her coming. Snuck right up on me— what was I thinking? Oh no, not again... Are we irritated, teacher?

Well folks, due to technical difficulties beyond our control, lunchtime will be delayed indefinitely...

The Main Man: 20 Years Later

This guy doesn't look as snobby as most of my customers, but he isn't saying much. Probably thinks I'm not as good as him or something. Some of them don't say a word—then they pretty much stiff you when you get to the airport. Can't even buy a pack of cigarettes with what some of these blowhards give you. Hot shot business types.

Last few jobs I've had haven't paid @#$%. No wonder all my credit cards are bumping their limits. If they'd really pay you what you're worth in this stupid country... but my wife doesn't want to hear that kind of talk. No, no, no. Prefers to rag on me about going back to school, so she can live in the style to which she's become accustomed with her daddy. At least this driving beats being in that apartment with her and that crazy kid...

Her old man's an idiot. Thinks I'm not good enough for her. Maybe a college degree would shut him up, but the thought of going back to school drives me insane. I tried it. One and one-half years of pure hell. They deliberately try to make it as boring as possible.

Here's the %#$% dispatcher again. "Where are you Jeff?", "Give me your location?", "Why is it taking you so long?" Why doesn't he get out here on the road himself with these other maniacs?

Move over you son-of-a-@#$%*! If you weren't so busy gabbing on your stupid phone, you'd be able to see where you're going!

This guy's a real chatty Cathy—two words so far. How did a jerk like him swing a house like he had? Won the lottery no doubt. Or maybe his daddy bought it for him. I'll tell ya, all I need to do is...

2

Symptoms

Attention Deficit Disorders are characterized by a common group of symptoms. There are different ways of grouping these symptoms, and some methods emphasize some more than others, so we will describe the ones that we pay most attention to in our work with ADD kids.

To complicate things a bit further, there is some disagreement in the field as to whether or not these symptoms constitute a "syndrome." That is, do they all have to go together, or can a child have some and not others? Some people have even wondered, for example, if it's possible to have a child who is hyperactive (gross motor restlessness) but who doesn't have an attentional difficulty. We do know that many investigators believe that it is possible to have a child with a concentration problem who is not hyperactive. ADD girls, we also know, tend to be less active than ADD boys.

A large percentage of ADD kids have *all* of the symptoms which will be listed below. It is also obvious that a good percentage of the children show only some of the ADD problems (we will specifically describe some of the major exceptions later). Children who might qualify for ADD with hyperactivity may show all of the symptoms listed below. On the other hand, *those who may be ADD without hyperactivity usually show symptoms 1, 6, and 8.*

Attention Deficit Disorder involves the different character- istics listed below. The first one, Inattention, is the most important or *Core* symptom. Symptoms 2-5 define the *Temperament*—or personality—that usually accompanies ADD (especially "with hy- peractivity"), and items 6-8 describe, in a sense, the *Results* of the other symptoms:

CORE	1. Inattention or distractibility
TEMPERAMENT	2. Impulsivity 3. Difficulty delaying gratification 4. Hyperactivity 5. Emotional overarousal
RESULTS	6. Non-compliance 7. Social problems 8. Disorganization

1. Inattention (Distractibility)

The ADD child has an attention span which for his age is too short. He cannot sustain attention on a task or activity, especially if he sees it as boring or semi-boring. Unfortunately, most ADD children spend a good deal of their time in school, and we hear from them over and over again how "boring" it is. Ask an ADD child what he doesn't like about school, and he may simply say, "the work." It is a significant strain for these children to try to stay on task; they are fighting an invisible problem they can't understand. The stress they experience is considerable and—for someone who has not gone through it himself—hard to even imagine. As they get older, ADD kids often begin to feel stupid, and they are often accused of being lazy. It is obvious that regular experiences like this are going to damage self-esteem.

What often confuses the picture here, however, is that many hyperactive children *can pay attention (or sit still) for limited periods* of time. Their ability to do this depends upon their being in situations that have one or more of four particular characteristics. These characteristics include:

1) Novelty
2) High interest value
3) Intimidation
4) Being one-on-one with an adult

This temporary ability of the ADD child to appear quite normal can appear quite amazing to people who have seen them in their hyperactive mode. It can also produce plenty of missed diagnoses! Examples of these unique situations? A visit to a doctor's office, watching TV, playing Nintendo, psychological testing, going to a ball game alone with Dad.

Another way of looking at the attention problem is to think of it as distractibility: the ease with which the child can be gotten off task by some other stimulus. Many ADD children can tell you how much it bothers them when other children talk around them, or when the garbage truck pulls up in the parking lot during social studies, or even when they have their socks on inside out.

Generally, distractors come in four forms: visual, auditory, somatic, and fantasy. Visual distractors are things within the child's field of vision that attract his attention away from his work or task. Someone walking by, for example, will cause him to look up, and then he may not return to his work at all. Auditory distractors are things the child hears that bug him. They can be obvious, loud noises, the ticking of a clock, someone else tapping his pencil on a desk, or another child sniffing. Keep in mind, these things may not seem bothersome to you, but they are to the ADD child.

Somatic distractors are bodily sensations that take away the child's attention. We have had a number of children, oddly enough, who have complained that when the seam in their sock is not in the right place they can hardly stand it, they become very fidgety, and can't concentrate well. Or if their stomach is growling, or the seat doesn't feel right, or they have a headache. Fantasy distractors are thoughts or images that go through the kid's mind that often have more appeal than things like schoolwork. We all daydream, but hyperactive children are often correctly identified by teachers as daydreaming too much. The child might think of his new video game, or about lunch, or—if he's old enough—about a girlfriend.

It may be true that some children are more vulnerable to certain kinds of distractors than others. Some kids, for example, complain more about things they hear than what they see. It also helps with the diagnosis if a child can describe in his own words what kinds of things get him off task.

2. Impulsivity

The second symptom that ADD kids often show is impulsivity. This means acting without thinking; sort of doing whatever happens to come to mind without regard for the consequences that will follow. Impulsive acts by ADD kids can range from trivial to extremely dangerous.

Several ADD children have caused their homes to burn down. One boy started playing with matches in a waste basket in his living room. The flames were intriguing, but they soon reached up to the curtains and then spread. No one was hurt in this situation, but the house was lost. Another five year old ADD child almost drowned when he went to a pool with his father one summer. The father turned away for only a short time, but the child saw the water, saw other kids jumping in, and thought fun. Fun! Period. His thought processes didn't extend as far as remembering that he didn't know how to swim. He was pulled off the bottom of the pool several minutes later, fortunately still alive.

Other impulsive ADD behavior borders on less damaging mischief. In school situations teachers will often recognize the ADD child by his tendency to blurt things out in class. Some of the blurting out may be an attempt to correctly answer a question, but the youngster forgets to raise his hand. Other times the child will blurt out things intended to be funny. Many ADD kids attempt to be the class clown, and, unfortunately, some of them are quite clever and really are funny. This type of behavior, however, presents the teacher with a major class management problem.

Impulsivity can also seriously impair the social interactions of the ADD child. When frustrated they can yell at other children, and sometimes even physically strike out or push others around in an attempt to get their way. Their impatience about having to immediately be the first in line, or their tendency to grab things can be constant sources of irritation to other kids.

One writer, Virginia Douglas, used to say that the ADD child had a "stop, look, and listen" problem. By this she meant that the Attention Deficit boy or girl, when entering a new situation, didn't take the time to stop, look at what was going on, listen to what was being said, and then respond appropriately. They just sort of bombed right in and did whatever came naturally.

In talking to ADD kids, one can readily get the feeling that they do not have a well developed ability to either visualize consequences or to "talk to themselves" about what is likely to result from some of their actions. Some ADD kids who impulsively steal, for example, just look at the money laying there and think, "Wow! Neat!" Then they take it. It may occur to them later that their father will almost certainly miss the five dollars that was sitting on top of the dresser in his bedroom, but by then the damage is done. ADD kids often lie for the same reason. They want to get out of the trouble *now*, and they don't think of what will happen later when they are caught. Parents are often totally amazed and mystified by this phenomenon. They can't imagine anyone being so "stupid" as to lie—not just once, but repeatedly—knowing they will certainly be caught later.

3. Difficulty Delaying Gratification (Impatience)

The third ADD symptom is difficulty delaying gratification. This is what you might simply call impatience. To the parents it feels like the child is saying, in effect, " I want what I want when I want it—which is NOW—and if you don't give it to me I'll have a temper tantrum or badger you to death until such time as you do decide to give it to me!"

When an ADD child gets an idea in their head about something they want, they can be remarkably persistent in pursuing it. This kind of behavior often makes shopping with them a miserable experience. Unless you're at a store where they have nothing of interest to the youngster, they can see a million things and want all of them in sequence. Some parents feel rather defeated about this before they leave home, and think that just about any shopping trip is going to mean buying the kid something. Long ago they gave up any desire to put up with the embarrassment of horrible tantrums in public.

At school, difficulty with delay can manifest itself in a number of ways. Shoving to be first in line is one, or running down the hall and bumping into people to be the first one out for recess. In the child's schoolwork, this impatience can show itself in hurried, messy work. To the child the task often is simply to "Get this stupid stuff out of the way as soon as possible," rather than to do a good job on it. Many times this can mean not reading directions and doing a lot of work the wrong way.

This characteristic of ADD can also result in sloppy handwriting. Since many ADD children do *also* have trouble with fine motor skills, it is sometimes hard to tell 1) if they are just rushing, 2) if they do have a problem with fine visual-motor coordination, or 3) if they have some combination of both.

Difficulty delaying gratification can also mean that birthdays are a pain, because the child gets so excited waiting and wants presents early. The times around Christmas and the holidays can also become difficult for the same reasons. Some children even have a lot of trouble with soiling or wetting because of difficulty with delay. This sounds strange, but it does happen. The youngster is out playing and is having a good time. He feels the need to go to the bathroom. You would think that with difficulty delaying gratification he would be more in a hurry to *go* to the bathroom, but unfortunately, it doesn't always work out that way.

What happens instead is that the child can't put off *the next few minutes of play*. He doesn't want to take the time out. The urge to go builds, he keeps repressing it, and then—in a moment of physical exertion—he loses control and soils or wets. Even after this, some kids will continue to play because they still don't want to go in!

If you think of this kind of mentality, you can perhaps easily imagine why one of the words that most frequently comes out of the mouths of ADD kids is "BORING!" If you were always obsessing about what the next exciting thing to come along was going to be—and in the meantime you feel like you're just sitting around and the minutes are crawling by, things might seem pretty boring to you too.

4. Hyperactivity

Hyperactivity is a very probable symptom of ADD, especially in the younger, preadolescent children. Parents will often describe the child as being always on the go, or "he looks like he's driven by a motor." Being around this constant activity can be very draining and very aggravating for parents, and repeated (but useless) suggestions to "Sit still!" or "Calm down" will be heard often around the house.

ADD girls, as mentioned before, tend to be less hyperactive than boys. Some studies have even shown that among normal babies in the hospital nursery, the boys in general move around more than the girls, so it isn't surprising that ADD kids follow suit. In previous years, as well, we had a diagnosis known as Attention Deficit Disorder *without* Hyperactivity. Also known euphemistically as the "pleasant space cadet" syndrome, this title was meant for a child who had difficulty concentrating but who did not present a lot of behavioral problems. These children *do* exist—some boys as well as girls, but among ADD kids they are in the minority and often fall through the cracks in the school system because they don't aggravate anyone too much.

Two other points bear mentioning. First, even among the

children who are often hyperactive, the hyperactivity will usually greatly diminish by adolescence. That doesn't mean the other ADD symptoms are gone. Second, hyperactivity is NOT constant; these kids can sit still in situations that are new, fascinating to them, somewhat scary, or one-on-one. There are only a few ADD children who can never sit still at all.

5. Emotional Overarousal

Another rather odd, but interesting symptom of Attention Deficit Disorder is an intensity of feeling that often goes way beyond the normal. It's as though the child cannot experience just a little bit of emotion. It always has to be a lot, and the ADD youngster will usually "broadcast" it, meaning that those around him will be very much aware of his state.

The two most common emotions involved here are 1) happiness or excitement, on the "positive" side, and 2) anger, on the negative side. A happy ADD child will often get into what we call the "hyper silly" routine, especially in groups of other children. He may run around, talk loud, act goofy, and generally make a fool out of himself. His parents may be mortified and the other children may look at him funny, but he doesn't seem to know or care that his behavior is inappropriate and overdone.

When angry, on the other hand, the child may produce a glorious temper tantrum. As mentioned before, these tantrums can sometimes appear as insane rages totally beyond the degree of frustration most people would experience. Because of these moments, many parents have felt their child was psychotic. However, the rage may subside as quickly as it started, and the child will be off to some pleasant, new encounter, leaving an exhausted and bewildered parent in his wake. Although emotional overarousal is usually thought of in terms of these two extremes, excitement and anger, it sometimes appears that in some children it can involve other emotions as well.

What other emotions are there? Anxiety, depression or sadness, and guilt. We have seen a few ADD kids, for example, who experience separation anxiety that borders on the phobic, and we have wondered if this reflects in them the tendency to feel everything too intensely. More common, though, is their tendency to experience sadness— and in older children depression—to a greater degree than normal. Fortunately, these periods of depression or sadness do not last so long in the younger children; mood changes are typical of ADD kids. However, as the child gets into adolescence a more pervasive depression is a serious risk, especially if the Attention Deficit Disorder—with all its primary and secondary symptoms—is not being treated effectively.

What about guilt? ADD children can probably have fleeting moments of guilt, but—according to most parents and as far as we can tell—this is not one of the emotions they tend to feel too intensely. Many of their parents wish they felt more! In fact, parents often worry that their child doesn't have a conscience.

6. Non-compliance

ADD children have a hard time following rules and they are usually significant discipline problems. Oddly enough, they can often recite and remember the rules during quiet times, but in the heat of battle they tend to forget—the emotional overarousal and impulsivity take over.

Much of the noncompliance involves aggressive behavior. The ADD child is often pushy with other children, and is usually terribly intolerant of siblings. These children, therefore, create an awful amount of domestic turmoil. Mom and Dad are often torn between their desire to treat their children fairly and equally and their knowledge that the ADD child does in fact start most—though not all—of the fights around the house. Other aggressive, noncompliant behavior includes arguing and yelling.

Passive noncompliance can also be a problem. Because of their general disorganization, forgetfulness, difficulty delaying gratification, and so on, ADD children don't clean their rooms, forget to feed the dog, and don't do their homework. One motto of our parent support groups is "Don't ever ask an ADD child to do three things in a row." You're lucky if he finishes one! A parent may ask the child to take out the garbage, and—if he agrees, which is unusual itself—he heads off to get it. On the way, however, he passes the TV. That's it—the garbage is forgotten.

7. Social Problems

Most ADD kids have a difficult time getting along with other children, especially those who are their own age. These difficulties will be elaborated further in the next chapter, but let us point out now that the ADD child's problems usually come from being too intense, bossy, aggressive, and competitive. ADD kids suffer from what is often referred to as "L.F.T."—Low Frustration Tolerance. Most of them hate losing, and they may resort to cheating, fighting, or changing the rules in the middle of a game in order to get their way.

This often results in the ADD child's being isolated or in their usually playing with children several years younger than themselves.

As we will see later, for many ADD children, social problems are a very big part of their life. It has been said that ADD with hyperactivity kids will often be *rejected*, while ADD without hyperactivity children will be *overlooked*.

Unfortunately, these problems are also very difficult to change, especially the bad reputation of the rejected child. This is especially heartbreaking and serious because one of the strongest predictors of adult success in life is one's social skills. Making matters much worse is the fact that social skills training for ADD kids doesn't work very well—at least so far.

8. Disorganization

If you had all the seven "symptoms" mentioned so far, you would probably have trouble with organization too, so this last symptom obviously overlaps with some of the others. Attention Deficit children are forgetful, lose track of time, and lose things.

There seems to be some innate psychological law which

dictates that trouble concentrating leads consistently to forgetfulness. ADD kids seem to forget everything. They forget what they studied just last night for today's social studies test. They constantly lose their schoolbooks, their clothes, the new watch, even their toys. What drives many parents crazy is an ADD child who doesn't do his homework. What really drives them nuts, though, is an ADD child who does his homework and then loses it before he even gets a chance to turn it in! This incredible feat has been done many times.

ADD children also have a poor sense of time and place. They can never seem to get home on time, even if they have a watch. Part of this, of course, is due to the problem with delaying gratification— they don't want to leave what they're doing and go home. But they also just don't seem to pay much attention to time. This is often painfully obvious in the morning when Mom and Dad are trying to get them out the door.

Fathers of ADD kids—and mothers to some extent—will find that the child is always borrowing their things, and then innocently losing them. These fathers will go through many sets of tools before the child grows up and leaves home. One little boy came in one day and his mother mentioned he had played a little league game the day before. When asked the score, the boy said, "It was 18 to 2." When asked next who won, he said he didn't remember! Normally one would recall vividly either getting killed by—or, on the other hand, murdering—another team.

ADD *with* vs ADD *without*

The biggest difference between ADD with hyperactivity and ADD without hyperactivity involves the Temperament symptoms. The "hyperactive" personality thought of here refers to the four symptoms of impulsivity, impatience, restlessness, and emotional over-arousal. Some people feel that ADD without hyperactivity children can also be impulsive, and perhaps there should be a sort of third category which includes mixtures of "with" and "without." It seems true in psychology that few diagnoses only have one, "pure" form.

Here are two charts that help organize and simplify our thoughts on these two diagnoses, but keep in mind that there may be many children and adults who do not neatly fall into only one category:

ADD with HYPERACTIVITY
(Most often a male)

CORE	1. Inattention or distractibility
TEMPERAMENT	2. Impulsivity
	3. Difficulty delaying gratification
	4. Hyperactivity
	5. Emotional overarousal
RESULTS	6. Non-compliance (Aggressive)
	7. Social problems (Rejected)
	8. Disorganization

ADD without HYPERACTIVITY
(Often a female)

CORE	1. Inattention or distractibility
TEMPERAMENT	Normal to lethargic
RESULTS	6. Non-compliance (Passive)
	7. Social problems (Overlooked)
	8. Disorganization

3

Effects on School, Home & Peers

The eight symptoms just mentioned often cause the ADD child problems in all areas of his life. It sometimes seems that the only time the child doesn't have any problems is when he's asleep. In this chapter we'll examine what an ADD youngster's life might be like. We'll assume that the child shows all eight symptoms, and that so far no one has either diagnosed the Attention Deficit or done anything effective about it.

School

Someone once said that if you maliciously set out to produce an environment that could daily drive an ADD child crazy, you couldn't come up with anything worse than school. This is probably true, because school requires that the youngster not only sit still but also concentrate on material that he usually finds uninteresting. "Boring" is one of the most common words used by ADD children to describe school.

Because of his difficulty with rules and self-restraint, the

ADD child is often a significant negative force in the classroom. He can stand out like a sore thumb, and all the other children will be aware of who he is and how much trouble he gets into. He will often get into a vicious circle with his teacher: he acts up, she tries to control him; he resists by acting up more, she attempts to exert more control, and on and on. By April, the teacher may just about hate the child and vice versa.

Even though his IQ can be the same as his classmates, the child's academic performance will be inexplicably uneven, causing adults to comment, "He can do it if he wants to!" He may be accused of daydreaming when he is distracted by internal stimuli, but at other times he may blurt out appropriate answers (but without raising his hand) or clown around making jokes or silly noises. Actually, most ADD children want to do well just as much as other kids do, and they can have spurts where they do well for periods of time. But because they are continually bumping their heads against this invisible concentrational problem, they will not be able to sustain their effort.

Some ADD kids have been known to have an entire year where they did not do all that badly. If this occurs, it is usually due to a very positive "teacher interaction effect." Bobby gets Mrs. Smith in the third grade. She kind of likes him, and she is willing to put up with a certain amount of goofing up. Bobby also likes her and is willing to work for her more than he usually does. The year goes fairly well. Mom and Dad start thinking Bobby is "maturing" finally.

Unfortunately, fourth grade rolls around and Bobby gets Mrs. Hammond. She doesn't particularly like him, and early in the year he impresses her as being kind of a brat. Bobby reciprocates, and in a short period of time the problems start up again.

What do we know about the IQ's of ADD children? ADD kids are probably about as smart as anyone else in general. That means some are quite bright, most are average, and some are below average. Some people tend to associate ADD with giftedness. Certainly there are Attention Deficit children who are gifted, but this is not typical. The problem with IQ, though, is usually that— whatever their IQ—ADD youngsters can't use all of it because of their difficulty paying attention.

With regard to learning disabilities, it's a different story. ADD kids as a group do have more of a tendency to *also* have learning disabilities. In the general population, perhaps 10 to 15% of all children have learning disabilities. In the ADD population, this figure may be more like 30 to 40%. These children, therefore, often have two handicaps to deal with.

The result of all these problems is that ADD kids will usually be significant underachievers, and from a very early point in time they will have learned not to like school. A typical conversation with an ADD child during a diagnostic evaluation may go something like this:

> "What do you think of school?"
> "I don't like it."
> "What don't you like about it?"
> "The work."
> "What's your favorite subject?"
> "Recess."

Some people believe that a child's "academic self-concept"—or what they expect of themselves in school—may be formed very early, perhaps by the third grade. This is a frightening notion, if it is true, because ADD kids will learn quite early on that school is not the place for them to be.

Home

Let's imagine that our ADD friend here didn't have such a good day at school. It would be nice if he could come home, put his feet up, and relax some. Unfortunately, it doesn't usually work out like that.

A hyperactive child will constantly bewilder his parents and will often become the black sheep of the family, just as he may have been the black sheep of the classroom. He will often be the source of constant disruption, and will produce what seems like an endless flood of noise. Sibling rivalry with ADD children is usually awful, with the ADD child most often being the instigator of the trouble. He is extremely jealous of siblings, sometimes correctly perceiving that they are simply liked more than he is.

General discipline is almost always a problem for parents with their ADD offspring. Nothing seems to work like it did with the other children. One study showed that out of every ten interactions between ADD children and their parents, nine were negative and only one positive. This obviously does nothing for anyone's self-esteem, and it produces a consistent burden for the entire household.

At home the ADD boy or girl won't seem to remember the rules or his chores. When asked to do even minor things, he may produce a major tantrum. He is usually sloppy, his room is a disaster area, and he doesn't follow through on things. Parents find that asking the child to do several things in sequence is usually a lost cause. After asking the youngster to turn off the TV, hang up his coat, and come to dinner, for example, parents may return ten minutes later to find the child still standing immobile—coat in hand—in front of the TV.

As the years go on, both the child and his parents can experience a continual drop in self-esteem and an increase in depression. Interestingly enough, though, the very first person in the family to get clobbered by the existence of an ADD child is not the child. *It is the mother.* The child is too little to really know what's going on, and Dad is out working with people who are hopefully sane, so Mom gets the brunt of the difficult child's behavior. And since we still live in a society that tends to blame parents for everything their kids do, the parents—and especially the mother—will constantly be trying to figure out where *they* went wrong with this kid.

Peers

As if these problems weren't enough, when the ADD child goes out and plays, he can encounter further difficulties. His frequent lapses in self-control make it hard to engage in games that require following rules and restraint. The ADD child suffers from a major case of "low frustration tolerance." Everything is a big deal to him, and he is extremely competitive, oftentimes trying to modify or create rules to serve the goal of winning at all costs.

As mentioned before, he will often be bossy and sometimes physically aggressive. Parents of ADD kids are often quite distressed by their child's treatment of playmates who come over to the house. The hyperactive child has a very difficult time sharing, and does not seem to pay much attention to what the other child wants to do. Many of these playmates don't want to return again, and the ADD youngster finds that they do not call to invite him over. It is not unusual for Attention Deficit kids to be left out of birthday parties that would usually involve their entire class from school.

Adding to the child's woes is their tendency in groups to get overstimulated and act "hyper" and silly, making stupid noises, poking people, and being a general nuisance. Since ADD kids are notoriously insensitive to verbal and nonverbal social cues, they will not realize how poorly they are coming across. Adults who try to tell the child to "calm down" in these situations find that their words are like throwing gasoline on a fire.

Though you wouldn't expect it with all these problems, ADD children often initiate interactions with other kids, but often in a negative or irritating way. One little third grade ADD girl would kick all the boys in the shins in the coat room at the end of the day. It was kind of her way of saying, "See you later," but the effects were obviously detrimental to her chances of getting along with anybody.

When the inevitable fights and arguments do occur, ADD children *always* blame the other kids for the problem. Parents waste their breath trying to point out to the child what he may have done to cause the trouble, even though the parent may have seen the whole thing.

The result of all these social difficulties is that the hyperactive child either winds up isolated or frequently plays with younger children. The cause for the isolation is obvious, but why do ADD kids wind up with younger playmates? There are several reasons. First, the ADD child's maturity level is usually several years less than his actual chronological age, so he fits in better in that respect.

Second, he will usually be physically larger than the younger children, so they will let him be the boss. This suits the ADD child just fine, and he will be much less frustrated if he always gets his way. Finally, this arrangement often suits the younger children just fine, too, because they find the ADD child entertaining and fun. He always seems to be coming up with something interesting to do. It may not be legal, but then again it's safe, because if they get caught, the older kid usually takes the rap!

This is not to say that it is bad for hyperactive kids to play with younger children. That is certainly preferable to having nobody to play with. Some of these children can also get along better with older, or opposite sex, kids. The acid test of the social skills of an ADD child, however, is their ability to get along with same age, same sex children.

4

Developmental Course

As they progress from babies to adults, ADD children will show different characteristics and behavior at different stages of their development. Though not all hyperactive children will show all the signs described below, the stages represent what you might expect in the growth of a child with full syndrome (all eight symptoms), untreated Attention Deficit Disorder.

Infancy

The infant signs listed here correlate to some extent with ADD, but they are not as reliable indicators as those that will be described later. There is a tendency for "ADD-to-be" infants to show more of a negative response to new situations and to simply spend more time in negative moods. (Apparently some people can be born crabs!) They can also show overly intense emotional reactions, disturbed sleep patterns, and feeding difficulties. Allergies are more frequent in ADD children, and the babies sometimes make strange, repetitive vocalizations. Finally, a few of these babies will physically resist affection and cuddling, almost as if they feel it is too restraining.

Keep in mind that these infant "signs" should be taken with a grain of salt. Many ADD kids were wonderful babies.

Toddlers

More reliable indicators of ADD occur when the kids get to be toddlers. In fact, many experts believe that it is possible to identify 60 to 70% of ADD children by ages two to three. The predominant indicators, though, will not include short attention span, because few two year olds concentrate on anything for very long.

Instead, noncompliance can become more of a problem and stubbornness may be extreme. If the child is a firstborn (and ADD kids may have a tendency to be more often firstborn), it is difficult for parents to tell if this is just the "terrible two's" or if the child is just "all boy." The child may walk early and always be on the go. Many of these children are accident prone, due to the hyperactivity, impulsivity, and the frequent coordination difficulties that many of them experience. They often stop taking naps at an early age—much to the chagrin of the mother—and are very demanding of attention, not playing well alone. If there are siblings, sibling rivalry and jealousy can be constant and extremely intense.

Ages Three to Five

As the ADD child gets older, noncompliance in public can become more of an issue, very often creating extremely embarrassing situations for the parents. Many families simply stop going out much, or even taking vacations, because of the awful scenes they have been through in cars, restaurants, and motels.

Peer problems can also emerge as the children graduate from parallel play to more interactive play, where the situational demands to share, listen, and get along are greater. Phone calls from preschools and kindergartens can begin about the child's misbehavior, often producing the beginning of "phone phobia" for mother. It is not unusual to find ADD kids who have already been "kicked out" of one or more preschools, often because of their aggressive behavior and difficulty complying with the normal routines.

At this age it also now becomes more obvious that discipline doesn't work with the ADD child like it does with other children, and frustrations may inspire "insane" fits of temper totally out of proportion to the actual difficulty. Hostile destructiveness is not uncommon in these children, but they can also break things or take them apart simply out of impulsive curiosity. At this point, too, Mom and Dad will start arguing more about how to handle the child, causing increased marital friction on a regular basis. The fact that these kids often respond quite differently to their fathers than to their mothers usually doesn't help the situation. A number of studies have shown the divorce and separation rates to be higher in families that have ADD kids.

Ages Five to Twelve

Now the ADD child hits the "big time" in school, where the demands to sit still and concentrate increase dramatically, and thus school complaints also become more frequent. In many schools these demands increase dramatically when the child hits first grade, so that is when many of the problems begin. Some kindergartens, however, seem to consider themselves junior versions of Harvard Law School, and they put considerable pressure on the children for self-restraint as well as academic performance. When this is the case, many of the ADD children will start having serious problems in kindergarten.

Retention is also frequently considered around this time because the "child is so immature." This should be given careful thought, however. Retention can often be a big mistake unless a complete ADD evaluation (see Chapters 7 and 8), IQ testing, and LD screening are done, because if the problem is primarily ADD, some of these kids will provide just as much trouble the second time around in first grade.

In the first, second, and third grades, LD problems may

begin to emerge, since a large portion of ADD children will also have a learning disability. It is very common for ADD kids to have major problems with handwriting, and for many of them this isn't just because they rush their work. It's also because their fine motor coordination isn't that good. Math seems to involve an unusual amount of sustained concentration, so it is often an area where many ADD children have difficulty.

Socially, the child may be more of a loner, and acting out can increase, such as lying, fighting, and stealing. Lying usually is related to unfinished schoolwork. Trends toward acting out are worrisome because we know that about 25% of our ADD children are at serious risk for later developing "conduct disorders"— problems that involve more serious, age-inappropriate and precocious activities that are sometimes illegal.

During the grammar school years the child is now old enough to know something is wrong. His self-esteem is beginning to suffer. Even though everything that comes out of his mouth is an attempt to blame parents, teachers, or other kids for his problems, he is now old enough to sense inside that something is wrong *with him*. He won't, of course, have the slightest idea of what it is, and may simply begin to feel that he is just dumb, mean, or weird.

Adolescence

Attention Deficit Disorder and adolescence don't mix too well. It's true that many ADD children will simmer down some in terms of gross motor restlessness, or hyperactivity, but much of the time ADD in the 13-19 year old crowd means "adolescence with a vengeance!"

By the time the ADD youngster is an ADD teen, many families are totally fed up and at the end of their rope after years of frustration. Other family members, especially fathers, can themselves get mad at the drop of a hat and at times outdo the child's tantrums. One of the things parents get so frustrated with is arguing. The ADD child has always had to have the last word for years, can never take "no" for an answer, and will argue endlessly over the slightest things. People who have lived in a home where this has occurred regularly develop an ability to "sense" a blowup coming, giving them an aggravating, disheartening, and sickening feeling.

Too many ADD teenagers are sick of school by the time they hit high school. Most will graduate, fortunately, but they will pay a price. Academically they may be behind their peers because of all the years when they couldn't concentrate enough to be able to learn what they were supposed to. Tackling high school courses with this shaky base on top of a residual attention problem is extremely difficult. Many of these kids long ago internalized the notions that they were "stupid" or "lazy," although they usually won't say this out loud.

Difficulties with peers can continue in adolescence, but they may not be as bad outwardly as they were when the child was younger, more aggressive, and more bossy. Isolation, however, is frequently a problem, or the teen may go through a series of short-term relationships that just never seem to last. One concern that often bothers parents is that their teenager does have friends, but the parents either don't like them or rarely get a chance to meet them. There is a danger that an unsuccessful ADD teen will hang out with the "burnout" crowd—those kids who also don't like teachers, school and their parents.

As you might expect, there is also evidence from some research that ADD teens are not as good drivers as their non-ADD counterparts. This is usually not such a horrible problem that one should not let them drive, but—when they're going out together—many parents try to get to the keys and to the car before their kids do. The reasons that ADD teens might not drive as well are fairly obvious. Imagine an ADD adolescent going to the store to get an exciting new tape and approaching a light that just turned yellow. Impulsivity, difficulty delaying gratification, emotional over-arousal, and noncompliance might all conspire here to produce a dangerous situation.

The picture is not all bleak, however, for many ADD teens. Some of them will experience a noticeable "mellowing" as they get older. Some of them are smart enough to do well in school and go

on to college. Some of them have friends who enjoy their exuber-
ance and their ability to be the life of the party. Some will go on to
find jobs where their intensity will be an asset. Parents find, though,
that ADD teenagers always seem to keep them somewhat off
balance.

Adulthood

We now know that ADD is not outgrown and that there are people
who are ADD adults, or what is sometimes referred to as "ADD,
Residual Type". Though this fact is discouraging, the situation is not
all bad. Symptoms like concentration difficulties, emotional overarousal, and even some forms of impulsivity can continue. On the
other hand, even though some symptoms continue, they do tend to
"mellow" out some, not being as severe as they were in the person's
younger years. It is also usually true that gross motor hyperactivity
will diminish quite a bit, perhaps partly because the adult has a lot
more pounds to maneuver around. In addition, a few lucky ADD
people—probably less than 40%—will show no symptoms as
grown-ups.

Though the symptoms mellow out some, secondary problems that were not part of the original ADD picture may now have
come along for the ride. "Growing up ADD" does not do a lot for
one's self-esteem, especially when 80 to 90% of the feedback you
get from your parents and teachers is negative. This can also lead to
depression and a generally gloomy outlook toward life and other
people. The ADD child usually had to sit through at least 12 years
of education, which required that he daily do two things which he
was never very good at: 1) sit still, and 2) concentrate on things that
were normally quite boring.

One significant blessing for many ADD adults is that there
is no more school! Unless, of course, by choice, but now there's a
difference. If you are ADD, you can go for yourself, if you choose
to, and you are no longer attending school primarily for the benefit
of your parents or for the society in which you live. You may also
choose something more interesting for you. The ADD adult may

also choose not to go to school anymore, and now may have a chance at picking an occupation that better suits his skills and temperament.

The personalities of some ADD adults may actually make them more effective in their work. Although a difficulty paying attention will never be an asset no matter what you are doing, some of the other ADD "symptoms" may actually help a person in some kinds of work. If you take someone who is reasonably intelligent and has good social skills, their intense energy level, strong emotions, and aggressiveness (appropriate) can certainly help them in certain jobs. Some will be good entrepreneurial types, and may succeed at starting their own businesses. They will do better in a situation where they don't have to have a boss. Others may do well at outside sales, where they can drive around or travel, meet different people, and use their energy making sales. The bad news for them? Occasionally they have to sit down at a desk and write their weekly or monthly activity or expense report.

Interestingly, there is evidence that ADD adults switch jobs more often, but also tend more often to have part-time jobs. This may be due to the unfortunate fact that their general socioeconomic status is lower than that of their family or peers, and perhaps they feel a need to supplement their incomes—or simply expend more of that excess energy.

The outlook here is certainly not all bad. Most ADD children, in spite of the fact that they maintain some of their symptoms, will grow up to be employed, married, physically normal, and self-supporting adults. And the problems that they do maintain can be treated (for more on ADD in adults, see Chapters 15-17).

5

Prognosis

A number of studies have shown that parental stress is usually based more on the parents' worries about how their child will turn out in the future than on what is going on right at the moment. When Johnny lies, steals, or pushes his sister to the floor, Mom and Dad will entertain very disturbing fantasies about his becoming a criminal, murderer, or winding up in prison. These worries, of course, vary from parent to parent, but they often take a very extreme form—imagining the worst—and they make parents very upset. Gronk.

Fortunately, although ADD is a serious problem, the future is usually not so bleak. The human mind, however, has a terrible propensity for repeatedly and automatically coming to the worst possible conclusions about a lot of things. Since we all seem to be natural worriers, therefore, it will be very helpful if we can look at some of the factors that can help us predict how the ADD kids will turn out later in life. Our goal here is to think as realistically as possible about the child's future, so we don't have to either dread it unrealistically on the one hand, or be too naive on the other.

Research on Attention Deficit Disorder has come up with a number of factors that have been shown to be related to adult outcome. Here they are:

I. Socio-economic Status

Higher is better. This may sound somewhat snobbish, but there may be several reasons for it. It may be that parents in higher socioeconomic brackets are better educated and therefore more aware of potential problems. They may also be more willing to seek assistance in evaluating a potential difficulty with their child. In addition, these parents will be more able to afford diagnosis and treatment, and to be able to continue it over the many years that it is necessary with an ADD child.

Finally, there may at times be some association between ADD and prenatal, perinatal, or postnatal difficulties. The child whose parents are in a higher economic bracket is less likely to experience danger here because his medical care is likely to be of higher quality.

2. IQ

Higher is better. A bright ADD child has a distinct advantage over less intelligent counterparts. Superior intelligence can go a long way toward compensating for many different handicaps, including attentional problems as well as learning disabilities. Since the worst place—in a sense—for an ADD child to be is school, and since performance in school is very much related to brain power, it is easy to see how a higher IQ can contribute to better prognosis.

Imagine for a moment two ADD children. One has an IQ of 100, which means exactly average and is the equivalent of the 50th percentile for his age group. The second ADD child has an IQ of 130, which is classified as "superior" and means he is smarter than about 97% of his own age group. (Keep in mind that an IQ is not a perfect pinpoint score, but only an estimate of the child's overall ability.)

Let's suppose, further, that these two children are in the same third grade class and are given the same math problem to do. Being ADD, they both have a fairly low frustration tolerance, and let's assume both of them can work on a problem for a maximum of seven minutes before getting frustrated and quitting. The ADD child with the 130 IQ finishes the math problem in four minutes, feels good about his accomplishment, and receives praise from his teacher. The ADD child with the 100 IQ, however, is capable of doing the problem in ten minutes, but this exceeds his frustration tolerance. After seven minutes of working, therefore, he gives up, starts bothering the child next to him, and gets in trouble with the teacher.

Quite different outcomes. Although the example is, of course, somewhat oversimplified, it gives a fairly clear idea of the advantage that IQ can provide. Multiply these experiences hundreds of times every year for each child, and you can easily imagine how the self-esteem of the two children would eventually vary.

3. Aggressiveness

More is worse. A large percentage of ADD children are overly aggressive in social situations. This can involve physical aggression—especially in younger children—as well as just plain bossiness. This characteristic, obviously, will turn off the child's peers as well as get him into trouble with adults. Prognosis is especially poor if the aggressiveness is not moderated with increasing age and if it turns into more serious forms of antisocial behavior in adolescence.

4. Hyperactivity

More is worse. Just as with the level of aggressiveness, the child who is extremely active will run into more problems than his less active counterparts. Although most hyperactive children can sit still in some situations that are novel, interesting, or intimidating, there are a few ADD children who can literally *never* sit still. Some, for example, cannot sit through a children's TV program where only a short attention span is required. As was mentioned earlier, most hyperactivity will be "outgrown" by adolescence, but those few children who don't outgrow it are in for more problems.

Ironically, there may be an instance where being less hyperactive is a drawback of sorts. This has to do with ADD girls. Since these girls are often not as active as the ADD boys and are simply kind of the "pleasant space cadet" type, they do not come to the attention of the adults who might be able to evaluate and help them. If they were somewhat more troublesome, they might attract some needed attention.

5. Social Skills

More is better. This is an extremely critical factor in determining the child's future happiness. Study after study has shown that a person's social skills play a major role in his adjustment. These studies have been done in many areas, not just with regard to ADD. Some studies, for example, have demonstrated that a simple thing such as "likability" is very important in the ultimate adjustment of a schizophrenic person.

With an ADD child we become very concerned if they have not developed some reasonable social abilities and do not have some friends by the age of ten. By this time it's getting late. If they are still isolated or arguing and fighting a lot with peers, they are in trouble. Playing with younger children, though, is still preferable to playing with no one at all.

Oddly enough, some ADD symptoms can off and on be assets for some children. The hyperactive older child can sometimes be the "life of the party" and enjoyed for his overarousal and high energy level, provided these qualities do not reach ridiculous proportions. Also, there is sometimes a fine line between bossiness and leadership. Some ADD children are capable of getting their way in a not so abrasive way, and this can be an asset. Maybe they'll run their own company someday!

6. Early Diagnosis

The earlier the better. Detecting just about any problem, whether it's cancer, a learning disability, or Attention Deficit Disorder, at the earliest possible stage is always preferable. Young children are still very malleable, and if their ADD is picked up in the preschool years and dealt with properly, they have a good chance to develop fairly normally and avoid some major self-esteem problems. Remember that we think we can detect 60-70% of ADD children by ages two to three. Trying to treat a 17 year old ADD child for the first time, however, is often very difficult because the child is so much more likely to be resistant.

7. Parental Psychopathology

Less is better. This is simply a rather fancy way of saying that the better put together Mom and Dad are emotionally and behaviorally, the better off the child will be. It does not mean that Mom and Dad cause ADD. But if the parents are fairly reasonable, competent, and intelligent—even though not perfect—the child will obviously be better off. Unfortunately, it is often hard for parents to show these qualities for two reasons: the stress the ADD child presents and the fact that biological parents of ADD children have a slight tendency toward certain types of psychological problems, which we'll discuss later.

Of course, healthy parents also make for a more stable family. A fairly strong family unit can do a lot in helping an ADD child develop more normally. If the child feels the parents and siblings are "on his side" and care about him, his self-esteem will suffer much less from the inevitable batterings he will receive. If Mom and Dad can negotiate their differences in a democratic and satisfactory way—especially as regards the ADD child, and if the family allows for open expression of thoughts and feelings, the child will be better off. One final but important sign of family strength that is very often overlooked is shared fun. The family that regularly plays together is always better off.

Looking at the seven factors listed will give some idea of how a child might turn out as an adult. It provides a sort of "risk evaluation scale." Not all the items represent fixed or unchangeable quantities, however, so this analysis can also help emphasize areas that still need work.

Seven Prognostic Indicators

1. Socio-economic Status
2. IQ
3. Aggressiveness
4. Hyperactivity
5. Social Skills
6. Early Diagnosis
7. Parental Psychopathology

6

Causes

Over the years there has been a good deal of controversy about what causes hyperactivity. Though the issue is not necessarily settled, there does seem to be a growing consensus about what might—and what might not—produce such a syndrome.

What Doesn't Cause ADD?

Experts for the most part no longer believe that bad parenting causes hyperactivity. Though marital difficulties and even abuse do cause problems, it does not appear so likely that they can generate the specific set of characteristics typical of Attention Deficit Disorder. We do not believe, in other words, that children *learn* to be ADD.

Unfortunately, however, this idea—"screwy parents make screwy kids"—is still the one most widely held in the society in which we live. Parents of ADD kids find it overtly or subtly expressed in the comments and reactions of friends, pediatricians, psychologists, teachers, relatives at the annual family picnic, and so on. The message is something like, "If you would only set firmer limits on this little brat, he would act like a normal child." Or if you drank less, or argued less, or spent more time at home, etc. This theory, which might be called the psychological, psychogenic, or family dynamic theory of ADD, obviously produces a great deal of unnecessary guilt in parents.

Actual physical brain damage also does not cause ADD problems in most kids. Only a small percentage of hyperactive kids show evidence of structural damage to their central nervous systems. Interestingly, also, less than 10% of children who do have hard evidence of brain damage show hyperactivity. These two facts are the main reasons why the old term "minimal brain damage" was discarded.

Contrary to Feingold's claims, diet does not produce Attention Deficit Disorder. Systematic research has consistently failed to support the idea that artificial colorings, flavorings, or natural salicylates are the nutritional troublemakers that produce ADD or LD in the majority of children. It may be true, however, that there is a small group of children that is diet sensitive in some ways, and parents' claims to that effect should never be taken lightly.

Also, contrary to popular belief, sugar doesn't cause hyperactivity either. Some interesting studies have shown that a child who OD's on sugar may actually become more lethargic for awhile— and also spacier. In other words, too much sugar reduces hyperactivity but also hurts concentration.

Similar to dietary effects in some kids, allergies may aggravate ADD, but they don't produce it to start with. Studies have shown, though, that as a group ADD children are more prone to allergies than the rest of the population.

What Does Cause ADD?

Current thinking favors two ideas that may somehow be related. One thought is that ADD is most often generated by a biochemical imbalance in the brain. There appears to be a deficiency in the brain's ability to produce or use certain chemicals called "transmitter substances," or neurotransmitters, which neurons (the electrical "wiring" of the central nervous system) use to communicate with each other and send messages. One neuron actually shoots these chemicals from little "buttons" across the gap between itself and another neuron, where the chemical may then be taken up. The theory is that a shortage of certain of these neurotransmitters results in the child's brain actually being *under*stimulated, and therefore deficient in regulating its own activities, such as attention.

There may be certain brain centers that serve a "governing" function, that is, they regulate the rest of the brain and the activities of the child in general. Imagine, for example, that the governor of a state was lazy, drank constantly, and spent all day in bed. The state itself would be a mess. People would fight, rob each other, not pay taxes. The schools, police, post office, and other services would be terribly inefficient. Chaos would result.

Perhaps something like that occurs in the brains of ADD children. The neurotransmitter deficiencies result in a "lazy governor," with the result that the child's activities are random, unfocused, disorganized, sometimes too aggressive, and generally too chaotic. One idea about why stimulant medications may work is that they "stimulate" these lazy governors to do their job correctly, with the result that the activities of the child as a whole become more focused, organized, and purposeful.

Theory Number 2

A second theory about what causes ADD was recently proposed, and the notion that ADD children are caused by screwy parents took another blow. Dr. Alan J. Zametkin published an article in the November 15, 1990 issue of the *New England Journal of Medicine* in which he identified a specific brain abnormality that may be linked to ADD.

Dr. Zametkin did his research with a team from the National Institute of Mental Health in Bethesda, Maryland. Among other things, the research studied activity in the brains of adults who had been hyperactive since childhood. What was found was that glucose metabolism in the brains of these people was significantly lower than normal, and that this lowered metabolic activity especially affected two keys areas in the brain that are known to be connected with the ability to pay attention and the ability to regulate motor activity.

Zametkin's study reinforced in a somewhat different way, therefore, the "lazy governor" notion described above. It also strongly supported the notion that stimulant medication treatment is not drugging children, but rather is treating a specific neurological disorder.

The study also brought up the fascinating possibility that certain areas of the brain that are known to play important roles in regulating attention and motor activities show unusually low rates of glucose metabolism in people with Attention Deficit. The "premotor cortex" and the "superior prefrontal cortex" were both less active, as shown in positron emission tomography (PET) scans, and this definitely goes along with the "lazy governor" theory. While overall glucose metabolism in the brains of these ADD adults was 8.1% lower than that in the brains of the normal control subjects, this lowered metabolic activity was even worse in these two areas.

Scientists, however, are always more cautious than parents when it comes to interpreting results, and this is as it should be. So while Dr. Zametkin's results are very encouraging, they are only a beginning. We still need for them to be replicated by someone else and for other areas to be explored.

What are some of the questions that still need to be addressed?

1) Will the same results hold true for children who are ADD? The subjects in this study were all adults, though all the ADD adults had ADD children.

2) Are other areas of the brain also involved in ADD, such as those involved in higher cortical processes that can also have some effects on inhibition and the regulation of activity?

3) How does medication affect glucose metabolism? Is this, in fact, how medications help, by normalizing this type of metabolism, or do they have some other mode of action?

4) Many people feel there are different "kinds" of ADD that may have different causes. Zametkin may have been looking at genetic ADD. What would the PET scans look like if the ADD population being studied appeared to have experienced prenatal problems of some kind, such as maternal alcohol use?

Even though there are still questions to be answered, Dr. Zametkin's study looks like a major step forward in ADD research. It will also continue to be seen as a support to parents of ADD children, and it will help further legitimize the use of medication in the treatment of these children.

Heredity and ADD

Other research has indicated for some time that Attention Deficit is also probably most often hereditary. The hereditary aspect of ADD is underlined by the fact that probably better than one-third of the parents of ADD children were ADD themselves as kids, and also the fact that the natural siblings and parents of ADD kids are more prone to certain emotional problems that the rest of the population is not.

While the overall prevalence of ADD in schoolchildren is thought to be around 5%, your chances rise to 25 to 30% if you have a biological sibling who has ADD. Biological parents of hyperactive kids also show a greater tendency toward certain psychological problems than the rest of the population. In addition to residual Attention Deficit, these parents also more often manifest depression and hysteria (especially in the mothers), alcoholism and sociopathy (especially in the fathers), and perhaps also psychosis and anxiety disorders. It is not always clear here, however, if these problems are in fact biologically based or the result of raising an ADD child.

Part II:

Diagnosing Attention Deficit

Diagnosis I:
Gathering the Data

The diagnosis of Attention Deficit Disorder is unique and often somewhat tricky in contrast to diagnosis in physical medicine or other types of psychological difficulties. The main reason for this is that, oddly enough, the direct observation of the patient in the office is one of the least helpful parts of the evaluation process. There are probably two main reasons for this. The first is that 80% of ADD children will not show their ADD symptoms in a doctor's office. The second reason is that many Attention Deficit children are simply lousy historians. They cannot accurately recall and/or describe their past experiences; others can recall, but are defensive and initially unwilling to admit any problems.

The result is that the diagnostic process involves primarily a lot of information collecting from sources other than the child. The child must also, of course, be seen, but what is needed primarily is qualitative and quantitative information about the child's school, home, and social functioning, gathered from multiple sources, especially parents and teachers.

Who can competently conduct an evaluation for Attention

Deficit Disorder? Actually any mental health professional or physician *trained in the evaluation of ADD*. A physician is not necessary. A physician does become necessary should stimulant medication be considered, just as a psychologist would be necessary when psychological testing is indicated.

The Diagnostic Process

We suggest that the evaluation process involve the following steps:

1. An interview with the parents first (unless the child is thirteen or over) to cover the presenting problems, developmental history, and family history, and to plan the rest of the evaluation procedures.

2. An interview with the child to get as much information as he is willing to give about home, school, and social functioning, and to rule out other possible problems such as psychosis or depression (which can sometimes be directly observed).

3. Some rating scales, such as the Connors Questionnaires, which describe home and school functioning and which can be scored using age and sex norms, and Barkley's Home and School Situations Questionnaires.

4. The collection of quite a bit of data from school, such as grades, achievement test scores, and current placement.

5. Psychological testing for IQ and LD screening is sometimes helpful, unless it has already been done by the school or someone else.

6. The contributions of the physical and neurological exams will also be discussed.

1. The Parent Interview

The child's parents are usually the most vital source of information and they should be taken very seriously. Approaching them with a nonjudgmental attitude is critical, and it is also realistic if the evaluator keeps in mind that it is very unlikely—if the child is

ADD—that the cause was faulty parenting. It isn't always easy to keep this in mind for several reasons.

First, many parents are so stressed by the child's behavior that they do not exactly make the best impression on the diagnostician. They can come across as angry, hysterical, depressed, or worse, and therapists with a strong leaning toward family dynamic theory will often conclude, "No wonder the kid's having such a rough time—anybody would with parents like these!" Many parents, however, will accurately report that they were not so emotionally disturbed and considered themselves fairly normal before the child arrived on the scene.

Second, there is evidence that the biological parents of hyperactive children as a group show a higher incidence of certain other psychological problems. These problems can include alcoholism, depression, hysteria, sociopathy, and psychosis. Further, since ADD is often hereditary and since it may be mostly found in males, the fathers themselves will often present with residual ADD symptoms. In an interview these men are often fidgety and very intense persons who frequently interrupt the interviewer.

Third, there is a higher incidence of marital dissatisfaction, separation, and divorce in families where there is an ADD child, so the couple may disagree and argue during the interview about the child as well as other issues. If only one parent is willing to come to the session, it will almost always be the mother, and she may show the effects of the stress resulting from living with not only one, but *two* ADD people—her son and her husband.

The first topic covered with the parents is, obviously, what brings them to the office. A general question about the presenting problems should be asked first and then, if ADD is suspected, more specific inquiries into other possible symptoms that may not have been spontaneously mentioned, such as emotional overarousal or difficulty delaying gratification. The presenting problems parents first mention usually focus on things like school underachievement, misbehavior, and domestic difficulties involved in living with the child.

Following a detailed analysis of the presenting problems, a

developmental history should be done. When an ADD screening is being done, this history should involve more than just the usual developmental milestones, such as when the child walked and talked. Since many writers feel that ADD symptoms can appear in 60 to 70% of hyperactive kids around the age of two, the interviewer should specifically inquire about the development of the ADD symptoms listed before, such as impulsivity, hyperactivity, impatience, emotional overarousal, noncompliance, and social aggressiveness.

It should be noted here that few parents will report a problem with short attention span in a two year old, since two year olds are supposed to have short attention spans. The interviewer is trying to focus on *age inappropriate* behavior. This is not easy, especially when the ADD child is a firstborn and the parents may have little perspective on what is normal for different ages.

Information about pregnancy, labor, and delivery are sometimes relevant, since there is a possibility that in some situations prenatal insults may produce ADD or something like it. Infant characteristics are not reliable predictors, but some writers have pointed out some mild correlations between ADD and infants with temperaments that involve negative responses to change or new situations, more time spent in a negative mood (including colic), and exaggerated emotional responsiveness. After three to six months, it is also suggested, the list of ADD infancy correlates can include resistance to cuddling, high activity level, sleep and feeding disturbances, and monotonous, ongoing vocalizations or crying. Keep in mind, however, that these are not extremely common or definitive signs.

After taking the developmental history, a family history should be explored due to the hereditary nature of Attention Deficit Disorder. Because of the preponderance of males with this problem, the father is usually "picked on" first with a question about how he did in grammar school. The focus here is often limited to things like concentration, grades, and misbehavior, because it is often difficult for people to remember that far back (especially males!). The mother is then asked similar questions. It is usually a good idea to explain to the parents why these questions are being asked, because this is often the first time many parents have ever even heard the notion that their child's problems may be hereditary and inborn, rather than a result of their faulty parenting methods.

Next, inquiries about other relatives, including siblings, are often helpful. The interviewer is looking for signs of ADD or residual ADD symptoms (especially in uncles), as well as signs of depression, alcoholism, hysteria, sociopathy, and psychosis. In very large families, reports of a few relatives with these problems should be temporarily taken with a grain of salt.

Finally, the initial parent interview should conclude with a joint planning of the rest of the evaluation and—if ADD is suspected—some way for the parents to learn more about this disorder (seminars, books, videos, etc.). This educational component is an extremely helpful part of the diagnostic process, because many parents will almost be able to make the diagnosis themselves after hearing more about the common problems and typical developmental course of untreated ADD. In addition, many of the fathers— and some of the mothers—will recognize themselves in the descriptions. This may lead to the possibility of treatment for them for adult ADD.

Finally, before they leave, the parents are given the Conner's Questionnaires and Situations Questionnaires to fill out and to take to the teachers. They are also asked to get the other school information, which will be described later.

2. The Child Interview

As mentioned before, when interviewing the child for the first time, the diagnostician should not expect to see hyperactive symptoms in the office. There certainly are some little ones who cannot sit still and who will be in constant motion as well as constantly chatty. These children will appear, however, only about 20% of the time. The goal of interviewing the child is to rule out more serious disorders, such as psychosis, see how willing the child is to talk, get as much information as is feasible about how the child feels about school, home, and social life, and begin to build a good relationship which may be necessary for later work.

We have found that the best way to begin the session with the child is to say in a matter of fact way something like, "I assume this wasn't your idea to come here." Most kids do not want to see any doctor, and this lets them know it's not unusual to feel that way. They will then usually talk much more freely. Most children will talk, though with widely varying degrees of accuracy as well as truthfulness. It is important that the interviewer not try to be too friendly—ADD children will frequently become very suspicious in reacting to an adult who seems too syrupy or condescending.

Older children can sit and talk for forty-five minutes to an hour, and many will open up quite a bit when confronted with an adult who is sincerely trying to understand them. Many of these children are so used to being criticized that this is a refreshing experience for them. With smaller children, having them draw or play while they talk is often useful, though the session may still have to be kept shorter, perhaps limited to one half hour.

When a child is too defensive to be able to tolerate sitting and talking about problems, several options are possible. One is to begin by talking about enjoyable topics or strengths; one little boy warmed up considerably while discussing fireworks. Some children are actually quite interested in the school information we collect, such as their old report cards or achievement test scores, and these can be shown to the child and often discussed very fruitfully.

Toward the end of the session, the child is also told—as are the parents—just what the rest of the evaluation process will involve. Some of the older children may even have some say in the design of that process. Some children, for example, are resistant to doing the Conners Questionnaire for school because they don't want anyone knowing they are seeing a "shrink." Other children may be interested in doing psychological testing if they think it might reveal some of their strengths.

3. Rating Scales

There are a number of good rating scales available for ADD, and different professionals have their preferences. The Conners scales are still probably the most widely recognized. The Parents Questionnaire has been revised to include 48 items which describe different child behaviors or characteristics. Ten of these are scored on a scale from zero to three, with three indicating that that item is "very much" a problem for the child. Therefore the best score is a zero and the worst score is a thirty.

Age and sex norms are available for this scale. This recognizes the fact that ADD is defined as age inappropriate behavior, and also that ADD girls are usually less hyperactive than ADD boys. The numerical cutoff, therefore, varies with age and sex. Scoring above it—according to the norms—indicates that the child is, in a sense, showing more difficult, ADD type behavior than 97% of the children of his or her own age and sex.

When using the Conners Parent scale, it is often useful to have the mother and father fill out separate scales, or make separate markings for their ratings on the same scale. One reason for this is that ADD children often behave much better with their fathers, who are often more intimidating and less familiar. When this difference between parents occurs, it is helpful to be aware of it in one's future work with the family.

The Conners Teacher Questionnaire has been revised to include twenty-eight items. Ten of these are also scored on a scale from zero to three, and age and sex norms for this scale are also available.

Also helpful are Barkley's Home and School Situations Questionnaires. These two rating scales approach the problem from a somewhat different angle. The Home Situations Questionnaire—filled out by the parents —lists sixteen different situations, such as "When at meals" or "When playing with other children." The parents indicate if this situation is a problem —yes or no—and, if yes, how severe it is on a scale from one to nine. The suggested cutoff for ADD here is simply more than 50% of the items checked as "Yes." The severity ratings are used only to provide more clinical information. As with the Conners Questionnaire, it is often useful to have mothers and fathers make separate responses.

The School Situations Questionnaire includes twelve items, such as "When arriving at school" and "During individual task work." The response format and scoring are the same as the Parents form. The School Situations Questionnaire is very useful, but has one limitation: it can only be used prior to junior high (sixth grade). The reason for this is that when a child has many teachers, as in junior high or high school, no one teacher has access to all the information necessary to fill out the entire form.

4. Other Data from School

The collection of other school information in addition to the current teachers' impressions is not always easy, but it is very important. Attention Deficit is a condition that starts early in life, so most ADD children will have had problems with school for a long time. Preschool problems are usually behavioral. Primary grade problems will often involve both behavior and concentration.

The first priority items we get are previous grades, all the way back to kindergarten, and the actual report cards, if possible. Many parents save these, and they are helpful not only for the grades themselves, but also for the teachers' comments. With ADD children, comments related to the basic symptoms are frequent and reappear year after year. These can include "always wandering around," "bothers others," "blurts out answers," "too easily gotten off task," and so on.

The grades of an ADD child are often extremely variable. We have had many children who—on the same report card—will get every possible grade from an "A" to an "F." This is due to the teacher and subject sensitivity of the ADD child, who can often function well if he likes the teacher and the subject, and who can go the opposite direction if he doesn't. However, it also is not unusual for the grades to vary tremendously for the same subject for the four quarters of the school year. (This drives parents and teachers crazy, and prompts them to come up with many creative theories about the effects of the seasons). In addition, since underachievement is a hallmark of the ADD child, the grades will usually not match the child's estimated ability level.

Achievement test scores are also gathered, going back in time as far as possible. The interpretation of these can also be somewhat difficult. Achievement tests are group administered, and ADD children usually do more poorly in a group than in a one to one situation. With many ADD children, therefore, the achievement test scores will not live up to overall ability. With others, however, they may not only be better than the child's grades for the same subjects, but may actually match the IQ.

This could be due to the fact that some of these children see this type of testing as intimidating or perhaps novel. This seemingly odd occurrence might also be related to the disappointing observation of many writers that achievement test scores do not improve after several years of medication therapy, even though grades do. Perhaps a good number of the ADD children did not do that poorly on these tests in the first place. If the child can remember taking these tests, it is often helpful to ask them if they recall really trying hard to do their best, or if they blew the tests off by impulsively guessing or by making designs on the IBM answer sheets.

The achievement scores, therefore, are more useful for clinical information than for discriminating Attention Deficit, although often the same striking inconsistencies can exist. We usually take the achievement scores to be a minimum estimate of the child's actual achievement as well as ability, assuming that IQ and achievement correlate reasonably well.

The child's current placement in school is also noted. If the child is in special education such as LD resource, we also collect the psychological testing and staffing information. This may make further intelligence testing and LD screening unnecessary.

5. Psychological Testing

Often (though not always) the intellectual potential (IQ) of the ADD child and the possibility of learning disabilities—in addition to attentional problems—should be evaluated. As far as other personality tests are concerned, projective tests are usually not worth the time they take and are not able to discriminate ADD in the first place. Vague comments about low self-esteem or hostility to authority figures are not especially helpful.

Intelligence. The intelligence tests normally used are either the Stanford-Binet, Wechsler Intelligence Scale for Children, or the Wechsler Adult Intelligence Scale (for older teens). A knowledge of the child's intellectual ability is important for several reasons:

A. The IQ tells us what we can reasonably expect from the child and to what extent he is underachieving.
B. The IQ is a necessary part of the definition of LD.
C. IQ is a major prognostic indicator with ADD.
D. Higher IQ levels can modify the ADD symptom picture by inhibiting hyperactive behavior to varying degrees at school.

Some writers have suggested that Wechsler scores may contain a "distractibility factor" that is reflected in the Arithmetic, Digit Span, and Coding subtests. Such a factor, if it exists, would certainly be important in evaluating the ADD child. While we do look at this trio of subtests, and many ADD children do drop in them, they do not powerfully discriminate ADD children from non-ADD kids. Although these three subtests do load together in factor analytic studies, the deficits in these scores do not necessarily have to reflect a concentrational problem in all children.

Learning disabilities. Since 35% or more of ADD children may also have learning disabilities, these should be separately evaluated. Difficulties involving visual and auditory perception or memory, as well as expressive language difficulties are unfortunately common. Handwriting problems are very frequently encountered with ADD children, though it is initially difficult to determine whether or not these are due to the child's impatience with schoolwork or to a fine visual-motor coordination problem.

As many writers have pointed out, however, the field of learning disabilities is an important part of American education, but it continues to be a service category characterized by inconsistency and disagreement. The model we use to define the presence of a learning disability is the standard score model. With this method, a learning disability is said to exist when there is a variation of more than one standard deviation (15 points) between an IQ test score and two other standard scores: 1) an individually administered achievement test score, and 2) a related processing score from an individually administered test. The scores must all be standard scores with a mean of 100 and a standard deviation of 15. A child, for example, with a Wechsler IQ of 103 who scores a 78 on a reading decoding test and 75 on a test of auditory memory would be classified as learning disabled.

The individually administered achievement tests include the Wide Range Achievement Test, the Peabody Individual Achievement Tests, or the Woodcock-Johnson Psychoeducational Battery. Tests of processing abilities, such as perception, sequencing, and memory, include the Detroit Tests of Learning Aptitude or the Illinois Test of Psycholinguistic Abilities.

A unique problem arises when we consider testing ADD children: *to what extent will the ADD itself artificially lower the tests scores?* It seems there are two types of ADD children here. The first type is capable of responding well enough in a one on one situation—where feedback of one sort or another comes every few seconds—that their scores are accurate. The second type of ADD child retains symptoms, such as distractibility and impulsivity, even in the testing situation, so that the scores become suspect. Although a competent examiner can observe these interfering behaviors during testing, it is hard to predict which children will show them and one runs the risk of the testing time being almost wasted.

There are two possible solutions to this problem. First of all, children who have a history of retaining their ADD symptoms even in one on one, novel, interesting, or intimidating situations may not be able to be tested right away. If it is thought that medication might be considered for them at some point, however, it might be started and titrated carefully before testing is done. Second, children who can inhibit their ADD symptoms in unique situations and maintain their self-control might be tested without medication, although this still might carry some risk. The psychologist doing the testing may be instructed to discontinue if they feel that too much ADD-like behavior is going to artificially lower the child's scores.

6. Physical and Neurological Exams

Just as there is no definitive psychological test for ADD, there is also no definitive physical test for Attention Deficit. It is certainly important, however, to know whether or not a child is in good health and whether or not their sensory apparatus is intact. Beyond this, the physical and neurological exams usually contribute much less than one would expect to the diagnosis of ADD. The role of an M.D. can be to exclude other possible physical causes, such as lead poisoning or thyroid problems, and to recommend other tests that may be helpful. As always, recent onset of symptoms versus chronicity of symptoms should noted, since ADD doesn't pop up suddenly.

A neurological extratg exam is not usually essential, although many people—who still tend to think in terms of the "minimal brain damage" idea—often feel that a referral to a neurologist is essential. The neurologist can often pick up what are called "soft" neurological signs, such as fine motor coordination problems, motor overflow, or perseverative behaviors. These, however, are only occasional correlates of ADD and can also appear in normal children as well, so their discriminative power in the diagnosis is not great. The same is true of the EEG. Though some ADD children will show some EEG abnormalities, such as an increase in slow wave activity, many ADD children have normal EEG's, so the test is not definitive. The EEG should not be routinely done for ADD evaluations, unless other problems are also suspected or present, such as epilepsy, chronic, severe headaches, or a recent onset of concentrational difficulties.

Essential Steps In Diagnosing ADD

l. Parent interview: presenting problems, developmental history, and family history

2. Child interview: home, school, and social functioning

3. Behavior rating scales describing home and school functioning

4. Data from school, such as grades, achievement test scores, and current placement

5. Psychological testing (sometimes) for IQ and LD screening

6. A recent physical exam

8

Diagnosis II:
Putting It Together

S ince ADD is not an all or nothing disorder—there are varying degrees of severity—and since there is no one definitive diagnostic procedure or test, the final determination of whether or not a child is ADD must rely on an integration of all the data collected. We suggest the following steps for making sense out of this mass of information. The diagnostician should also keep in mind that they are attempting to describe a profile of strengths and weaknesses for this particular child, in addition to a statement about the presence or absence of ADD.

Eight Integration Steps

Step 1: Matching the presenting problems with the eight ADD symptoms listed in Chapter 2, such as short attention span, impulsivity, hyperactivity, difficulty delaying gratification, emotional overarousal, and so on. We also look for school underachievement and social problems that usually involve being too bossy or aggressive. Correlates of ADD are also examined, such as allergies, fine and gross motor coordination problems, and minor physical anomalies.

Step 2: Matching the developmental history with what we consider to be the typical course of untreated Attention Deficit Disorder (Chapter 4). This involves, of course, looking for the manifestations of the various symptoms listed above, but also being aware of how the picture changes with age. Early hyperactivity, for example, will often be outgrown. Self-esteem and depression issues do not usually become significant until after age seven or so. Retention in school is common in the early years, but has been known to occur with some ADD kids as late as junior high school.

Step 3: Checking the family history. The single most frequent indicator here, which we weight heavily, is what is often called the "chip off the old block syndrome." If the father especially says that he was very similar to the child when he was in school, and this is said without much doubt or hesitation, we consider it strong evidence for genetic transmission in this case. A previously diagnosed ADD sibling is also a strong indicator, because it raises the chances of ADD in the child being diagnosed from about 5% to about 30%. The possibility of an ADD mother also cannot be forgotten, especially since the sex ratio with ADD is now rather unclear.

Step 4: Is the information from the child consistent with the usual ADD symptoms? Consistency here can mean two things. Some ADD children can and do describe in their own words typical symptoms. Those most often described accurately include distractibility and sometimes emotional intensity; the others are not as often mentioned because the child sees them as weaknesses, such as with hyperactivity itself. Other ADD children manifest ADD symptoms indirectly through other types of comments, such as saying they hate school "because of the work" or consistently blaming other people—teachers, playmates, parents—for whatever problems they have. It is important to keep in mind that about 20% of these children will show hyperactive kinds of behavior in the office, such as fidgeting, interrupting, and being distracted by the various objects in the room.

Step 5: Does the child score above the cutoffs for the Conners (or other) Questionnaires according to the age and sex norms?

Step 6: Are more than 50% of the situations checked as problems on the Home and School Situations Questionnaires? How severe are the ratings?

Step 7: Does the school and testing information support the notion that the child is not working to capacity? Also, to what extent are learning disabilities accounting for this underachievement if it exists?

Step 8: Do the parents—after becoming familiar with an ADD seminar, book or an educational video—feel their child is Attention Deficit? Most of the parents who say "That's my kid!" are correct.

Idiosyncratic Patterns

Many children will "test positive" for ADD according to all eight steps. The diagnosis is then made and treatment planning proceeds according to the specific strengths and weaknesses of the individual child. Other children will definitely not be ADD, or will present a more ambiguous picture. There are several unique factors that can make substantial changes in the typical symptom picture, and which may at times cause the diagnosis to be missed in a genuine ADD child. These factors include the following:

1. Good social skills. A significant number of ADD children will get along well with their peers. They will have friends, not be particularly bossy, and may not show the usual low frustration tolerance in competitive situations. In some of these children some of the ADD symptoms are moderated just enough to become social assets. Bossiness, for example, becomes leadership, or excessive energy makes the child the "life of the party."

2. High IQ. ADD children who are smart enough can not only succeed in school, but may also actually enjoy it. Because of their academic success and the reinforcement they may receive from parents and teachers, their inappropriate behavior may be inhibited while at school. However, many of them will go off like rockets when they come home, and then a number of hyperactive symptoms will appear there routinely. This often leads many observers to incorrectly conclude that the family itself is the problem.

3. Shyness. From the earlier descriptions of ADD children, they sound anything but shy. Instead they often seem uncaring about how others see them and socially boorish. There are, however, a few ADD kids that are the opposite and are extremely concerned about the opinions of others. They consequently inhibit in public their hyperactive behavior, but—like the high IQ child—they will usually show ADD symptoms at home. Some of these children have become quite shy because of major coordination or speech difficulties that in their earlier years made them the targets for a lot of ridicule from peers.

4. No siblings or one-on-one preschool situation with parents. In a few children who are hyperactive, their problems will not appear until they reach school, such as kindergarten or first grade. When taking the developmental history with the parents, one will not get reports of extreme hyperactivity, impulsivity, over-arousal, and so on. The reason for this is occasionally the lack of siblings at home during these years. Apparently the lack of competition, in addition to having reasonably competent and attentive parents, can produce fairly normal behavior, at least for a while.

5. ADD without hyperactivity. Although the last diagnostic manual eliminated this category, we still feel it is legitimate. When hyperactivity is not a problem in the early years, many of the other possible symptoms, such as emotional overarousal and social aggressiveness, also tend to be moderated quite a bit or just plain nonexistent. When this is the case, *the diagnosis must focus heavily on the existence of a major concentrational difficulty itself,* and on its showing up in persistent passive noncompliance and disorganization.

ADD vs LD

One last diagnostic problem should be mentioned: the difficulty discriminating ADD from LD. These two categories often overlap, but there are children who can have one handicap and not the other. There are several ways of attempting to discriminate Attention Deficit from learning disability. The first is the developmental history. Most LD-only children will not show at age two or three many ADD symptoms such as hyperactivity, impulsivity, emotional overarousal, social aggressiveness, and so on.

Second, if the child's IQ and achievement are not discrepant and the tests or other measures are considered valid, LD can be fairly well ruled out by definition.

Third, if from the early school years on, there are consistent comments about distractibility itself and short attention span, one leans more toward ADD.

Finally, a medication trial can often eliminate a lot of ADD symptoms. If the medicated child then appears normal, and shows no academic handicaps or underachievement, it would appear that the problem was ADD alone. It is not generally thought that medication will remediate a true learning disability.

Careful!

A valid diagnosis of ADD may
be missed in children with:

1. Good social skills
2. High IQ
3. Shyness
4. No siblings
5. No hyperactivity

Part III:

Multimodal Treatment of ADD

Multimodal Treatment Checklist

√ 1. Education about ADD
√ 2. Counseling
√ 3. Social Skills Training
√ 4. Parent Training in
   Behavior Management
√ 5. Medication
√ 6. Parent-School Collaboration
√ 7. Classroom Management

9

Education and Counseling

Educating anyone who is going to be affected by ADD in a major way is very important. Teachers, mental health professionals, and pediatricians must have a good working knowledge of the facts about basic symptoms, developmental course, causes, prognosis, diagnosis, and treatment. Siblings, grandparents, some friends, and babysitters should also come to know more about this disorder if they have regular contact with the ADD child. And, of course, the most important people to teach about ADD are the parents and the child. Parents should become "experts" in ADD, and the ADD child should be given information about the disorder that is presented in language and concepts that are appropriate to their age.

Issues that should be covered involve specific facts about Attention Deficit Disorder, from symptoms to side effects possible with certain medications, to reasons for various interventions selected with the child. If the boy or girl is going to an LD resource special education class, for example, they should know that it is to work on their writing and math skills. They should also know how long they are likely to be in it, and what the criteria are for getting out of it. Education about some of the emotional issues that come along with ADD treatment should also be discussed. If the child is into a period where he doubts why he has to continue taking medication, when a good friend of his just stopped it, it is helpful for him to have some objective person—perhaps outside the family—who can listen to the child first and then gently provide the needed answers.

Parents should, of course, first become educated about ADD and then help to pass along information to their child as the youngster becomes able to understand it. A good guideline or checklist for the kind of information that Mom and Dad need to assimilate is the Table of Contents of this book. From the definition of ADD to diagnosis to adult ADD, all the information is critical. It also must be gone over again and again, since it is impossible to learn it all the first time around. Although this field is not known for sudden or dramatic changes, one must also be on the lookout for new developments.

Education and Counseling Work Together

It's easy to see from this discussion that educating people about ADD can evoke a good deal of feeling. It can also affect people's thoughts about themselves and about the whole treatment procedure. Therefore, this education is certainly going to be intimately involved with—and sometimes indistinguishable from—psychotherapy or counseling as those ideas are usually thought of. Three important and helpful examples of this kind of "education/therapy" include 1) the "no-fault" notion about cause, 2) the Symptom Rating Scale, and 3) self-esteem reevaluation.

1. The No-Fault idea. When someone explains to you that ADD probably has a hereditary base to it that no one in the family—child or parent—could have changed, they are essentially saying that ADD is no one's fault. The "no-fault" idea has two major implications. The first is that Mom and Dad do not need to crucify themselves with guilt about what they think they did to produce the bad behavior of their offspring. The guilt they have been feeling, however, is somewhat tenacious and doesn't just suddenly evaporate, so it becomes the job of continued counseling to learn, practice, and reinforce correct ways of thinking until they become more habitual. More reasonable and less painful feelings will then come along for the ride.

The second implication about attributions of fault is that the ADD wasn't the child's fault either. He did not grow up with the idea of torturing his parents at every opportunity and he was not put on earth to make them miserable. This idea can somewhat reduce the amount of anger that parents feel toward their little ADD one, but it won't get rid of it all. ADD kids are still too obnoxious too much of the time. The idea is also not to be used as an excuse by the child for his behavior. Suppose one day, for example, his parents confront him while he is sitting on top of—and pounding on—his little sister. He responds by saying, "What can you expect? I can't help it because I'm ADD and have a problem with emotional overarousal and impulsivity!" This doesn't cut the mustard. It's an excuse and is irrelevant. Discipline should still follow.

2. The Symptom Rating Scale. It is obviously important for ADD children and parents to know what the basic symptoms of ADD are. ADD, though, doesn't affect all children the same way, and it comes in different forms and degrees, so it is also essential for particular children and their parents to understand which symptoms they are going to have a harder time with and which ADD characteristics are milder or even nonexistent. One way of accomplishing this education/therapy task—and of perhaps killing two birds with one stone—is to make up a "Symptom Rating Scale" (page 85).

With the Symptom Rating Scale (SRS), both the kids and the parents can rate, on a scale from 0 to 10, to what extent the child manifests each of the eight ADD characteristics (symptoms) described in Chapter 3. The ratings should be done separately by the child and by each parent, so each is not biased by the others' responses. Siblings, other relatives, teachers, and other involved parties can also do ratings. It is often helpful to also indicate on the SRS what situations in the child's life either aggravate or ameliorate a particular aspect of the child's behavior.

Doing the ratings helps the child understand how ADD affects him. It helps his parents know better what to expect, and to keep their expectations realistic as they struggle to "think ADD." Thinking ADD means not expecting a handicapped child to behave like a normal child, but also being ready to manage the difficult behavior when it comes. If the child and family are working in counseling with a therapist, the ratings can be discussed openly. Differences in ratings among people are often important to look at (if, for example, Mom rates things a lot worse than Dad), and the ratings naturally lead to discussions about how everyone—child, parents, and others—can better handle problems when they occur.

3. Self-esteem work. Many people feel that the real bottom line in our lives is a psychological/emotional one: our self-esteem. Self-esteem affects not only our general mood, but also how much satisfaction we get from being alive. What we think of ourselves is obviously affected by what happens to us and how we do in life, but as we get older and older a strange thing often occurs. We begin to develop a more and more permanent view of ourselves that, oddly enough, can become somewhat independent and separate from what is actually happening and from what we are really doing.

This wouldn't be so much of a problem if the self-esteem of people were unrealistically positive. If that were the case, people would be able to perform rather poorly but still feel good. They would be able to ignore their faults, though this probably wouldn't help them much when it came to correcting their behavior.

It is probably more common, however, that people overemphasize their faults and ignore their good points when evaluating themselves. If, in the course of a day, they do eighteen things right and two wrong, they stew at night about the two things that were goofed up and they forget about all they accomplished. This leads, obviously, to a negative self-concept, but it also can help generate depression.

What negative things—in relation to themselves—do parents of ADD children distort or overemphasize and what positive things do they forget? Parents often feel guilty because of repeated irritations with the ADD child and the feeling of "I don't love or even like him!" Parents also feel guilty when they come up with the common—and distorted—question, "What did I do to cause all this kid's problems?"

Positive things forgotten by parents include all the work they do daily just helping to keep the kid afloat. This includes the mundane operations of driving, cooking, laundry, and purchasing necessities like toothpaste and clothes. It also includes the harder tasks that go along with having a handicapped child, such as going to staffings, seeing counselors, and putting up with large doses of embarrassment at family picnics. No one will give anyone a medal for these things, but perhaps they should. Reorganizing the way you think about yourself can be very helpful to maintaining your self-esteem at a reasonable level.

Counseling for the Kids

Individual counseling. There is some controversy about the use of counseling with ADD children. Most people feel, quite justifiably, that ADD kids are very much in need of counseling or psycho-therapy. Others point out, however, that the very symptoms that make children ADD also make them poor candidates for counsel-ing. The ideal therapy candidate, for example, is not usually thought of as someone with a short attention span, a tendency to blame everyone else for their problems, and no desire to see a therapist in the first place.

Yet it is important for the ADD youngsters to see someone periodically as they are growing up, and the visits certainly do not need to be weekly. The counselor may serve several functions: support, education, and mediation. In a world that seems to be continually critical of their every action, an ADD child's having someone who listens sympathetically and points out their good qualities can be like a breath of fresh air. The therapist can also help educate the child about Attention Deficit, and it is often much better if this information comes from an outsider rather than one of the youngster's parents. And finally, from time to time the counselor may be able to help mediate disputes between the child and their parents, covering issues such as homework (at age 10) or the use of the car (at age 17).

Even though it may be true that ADD kids do not make the best counseling prospects, children vary a lot, and some are better therapy candidates than others. How can you determine the extent to which an ADD child can benefit from individual therapy? Several factors may give you a rough idea. First of all, the age of the child is obviously important; a twelve year old is much more likely to benefit than a six year old. Second, how well can the child relate to or get along with this particular professional? Sometimes the "chemistry" is pretty good. Third, how defensive is the youngster about discussing their problems? Some kids won't touch them with a ten foot pole, while others are much more candid and open with a sympathetic adult.

If an ADD child appears to be a good candidate for therapy, other kinds of assistance might be considered. These include self-control training and social skills training.

Self-control training. Sometimes referred to as CBM—cognitive behavior modification—self-control training takes the point of view that the ADD child's difficulties with self-control result from a lack of an internal language that a normal child can use to talk to himself, in a sense, and thus anticipate the consequences of his actions. Some CBM techniques, therefore, try to teach the ADD child how to create and use this internal dialogue. The therapist, for example, may ask the child to say out loud, "If I talk to the kid next to me in class, I won't finish my work, may get a detention, and may have to stay after school." Then the child whispers the same words, and eventually he just says them to himself in his head. The therapist then tries to encourage the child to actually do this in the classroom: to stop and think instead of acting impulsively.

Social skills training. Social skills deficits can result in widespread problems, including poor school performance, social aggression or withdrawal, and adult pathology. Social skills building is based on the assumption that adjustment problems are related to deficiencies in abilities and that correcting or learning these skills will result in fewer serious problems.

Current work in this field involves systematic training approaches that provide for the introduction and mastery of individual skills in a supportive environment and, hopefully, the generalization of these skills to other settings. This approach holds that the most straightforward treatment is to 1) tell the child what to do in situations identified as problematic, 2) show him or her how to do it, and 3) have the child practice the skill before using it in real life. Parents and teachers can then take advantage of opportunities to strengthen the new behavior.

What exactly are social skills? Some of these things may seem obvious or simple to parents who themselves are already able to do them, but they are not obvious to many ADD kids. They include things such as:

1. Following directions
2. Giving and receiving positive feedback
3. Sharing
4. Compromising
5. Dealing with name calling
6. Sending an ignoring message
7. Joining a conversation
8. Problem solving
9. Saying "No" to stay out of trouble

In a social skills training group, these different behaviors are discussed and then practiced. Children are reinforced regularly for their cooperation, and during the group session there are often frequent breaks. Because generalization is always a concern, "homework" assignments are frequently given to the child in the social skills group. It is also helpful if parents and teachers are informed of the skills being learned, and suggestions given to them for reinforcing this behavior in the school setting. Since ADD kids don't usually remember on their own to try to do things differently in different situations, having an adult present who can signal them when it's time to try something new—and reinforce their attempt afterwards—can help a lot. This is especially true since there is no guarantee that other children will provide reinforcement, and an ADD child who already has a bad reputation will find it very difficult to change.

Social skills training still remains a very difficult undertaking, and results are hard to come by. Some of the more successful programs are very "labor intensive," meaning that quite a few trainer/supervisors are necessary for each child in order to cover as many situations as possible. Even with this type of help, one can't be with an ADD child all the time, and spontaneous, "uncovered" social interactions may still too often be negative. The critical importance of social skills for the child's future, however, makes this an area that we must continue to aggressively explore. Perhaps in the future new ideas, such as the use of video training or peer "guides," will make significant inroads into this heartbreaking dilemma.

Counseling for the Parents

Very often an essential part of the multimodal treatment package aimed at helping the ADD youngster involves individual and/or marital counseling for the parents. The stress of raising—and of just living with—an Attention Deficit child takes a lot out of a parent, especially a mother, and it also places a constant burden on the relationship between Mom and Dad.

Individual counseling. As mentioned before, parents of ADD children show, as a group, a higher incidence of depression, alcoholism, hysteria, sociopathy, anxiety disorders, psychosis, and residual ADD. This list, of course, sounds pretty bleak, but keep in mind that any one parent isn't going to have all these problems and many parents will have none of them. When counseling is indicated, however, it can help immensely with a parent's individual adjustment. Often it will also help stabilize the marriage and the family, thus providing more support for the child.

Many adults find what is known as "cognitive therapy" especially helpful. With this approach a person takes a long hard look at how they think about things, and attempts in the process to make their thinking and perceptions about life and other people more realistic. Cognitive therapy is based on two notions. First is the idea that one's emotions are greatly affected by how one thinks about things. Second is the idea that when a person is extremely upset about something, it is usually true that their thinking is distorted. With the help of a therapist, many parents are able to "rethink" things and sort of get back to reality, with the result that they gradually train themselves to feel better.

Cognitive therapy certainly doesn't take away all the pain, but it can make quite a dent in it. It is also often helpful for Mom or Dad to consider using some of the "psychotropic" medications that are available. Most parents are quite ambivalent about the idea of their taking medication—just as they were when they considered it for their child. As often happens with the children, though, the effects of medications such as antidepressants and minor tranquilizers can be truly amazing. A good therapist will carefully explain the possible benefits as well as possible side effects of the different drugs available before a trial of any one medication is begun.

Marital therapy. As mentioned earlier, the divorce rate appears to be higher in families that have ADD children. This results not only from the stress of having an ADD child, but also from the problems (listed above) to which parents of ADD kids are more vulnerable. Fortunately, research has shown many times that marital counseling can be of significant help.

One method of marital counseling that is very helpful involves a combination of cognitive therapy and negotiation training. This can involve several steps.

Step 1: Evaluation. The therapist may meet with the couple first to get some idea of the "state of their union" and to find out how interested and willing they are to work on it. The conjoint session is often followed by individual sessions to explore these issues in more depth and to cover things that each person may not be comfortable discussing in front of their spouse. During the evaluation process, the therapist and clients evaluate which issues are causing the most trouble. These often include things such as:

1. Communication
2. Management of children
3. Money
4. Sex
5. Social life
6. Work and work schedules
7. Fun (or lack of it)
8. Alcohol and drug use
9. Jealousy
10. Values and religious beliefs

Step 2: Introduction to cognitive therapy. Couples are trained regarding how to think about themselves and their spouses more realistically. This includes things such as learning how to stop blaming one other, how to think more realistically about oneself, and how to take responsibility for one's own anger or depression.

Step 3: Negotiation training. Many—if not most—couples are not too good at talking things over in a way that is productive. Having an ADD child running around the house wreaking havoc half the time doesn't help either. Unfortunately, many men and women fall into the "avoid it or argue about it" routine, and significant problems go untouched for years.

Some attention to and assistance with basic negotiation procedures is often necessary. The therapist can help a couple master some straightforward, though difficult, communication/negotiation methods, such as:

1. Agreeing on a time and place to talk
2. Defining clearly the problem to be discussed (one at a time, please!)
3. Letting each person express their opinion without being interrupted
4. Sympathetically listening, rather than simply preparing a rebuttal
5. Generating possible solutions

6. Agreeing on something to try out

Step 4: Getting it together. After having explained themselves to each other and to the therapist, and after some orientation to straight thinking and negotiation skills, Mom and Dad can get on with the job. This consists of taking each problem identified and doing two things with it. First of all, straightening out one's thinking about the problem, and second, applying the negotiation methods to it in order to come up with a solution. The therapist comes along for the ride to try to prevent anyone from lapsing back into things like useless arguing or thinking of the other person as an idiot. It's hard work, but it can help a lot.

Controversial and Idiosyncratic Therapies

One of the problems in any area of physical health, mental health, or just health in general is trying to determine just what kinds of treatments work with a particular problem. Unfortunately, it's possible to hear of many different kinds of treatments that "work" for many different kinds of problems, but in the fields of psychology and psychiatry especially, there are many more claims of effectiveness made than there are legitimate approaches.

This is partly due to the fact that "placebo" effects are more rampant in these fields than in physical medicine. Placebo effects occur when someone apparently "gets better" because they think they are being treated with an effective procedure. Such effects usually don't last very long, but they can provide ammunition to many frustrated people who want to climb on the bandwagon of some supposedly hopeful new way of doing things. When it comes to ADD, these placebo effects apparently can also be passed on from parents to kids. It may be that parents who are willing to go to the trouble of trying some new kind of diet, for example, also inadvertently do a lot of other things that may—at least for a while—help their child do better.

How can you tell if a kind of therapy is not really one that will work? Generally, unless you're willing to read all the literature and go to all the conferences on the subject, it's quite difficult. You almost always have to rely on someone else's opinion. If you're a parent, you pretty much have to rely on the professionals; and even if you're a professional, you still have to rely on other professionals.

Fortunately, professionals fight a lot and don't always agree with one another. What is good about that is that if somebody comes up with an idea about something, it had better be able to stand the test of time. Other professionals—even those who didn't develop the idea—must also come up with the same opinion. All this hassling back and forth is published in professional journals. Some of it may sound tedious and petty, but after a while it's possible to get a sense of the "state of the art." Those things that stand the test of time will be recommended and will work, according to scientific literature that involves carefully designed and controlled studies. Other approaches will fall by the wayside or will eventually fall into the "Controversial and Idiosyncratic Therapies" category.

How do you know if something falls into this category? It's not always easy, but there are several ways to tell. One is that the theoretical backup of the method doesn't fit with modern scientific knowledge. Another is that the technique may be claimed to be effective for a broad range of rather poorly defined problems. Adverse effects are often minimized since the therapy may emphasize "natural" methods such as diet, vitamins, or bodily manipulations. The initial presentation of the therapy may appear in the media rather than in scientific journals, and later controlled scientific studies that don't support the method will be discounted due to "bias" or the alleged unwillingness of the scientific community to accept new ideas.

What are the controversial and idiosyncratic therapies as of now? To date, there are no reliable indications that such approaches as biofeedback, a food-additive-free diet, elimination of sugar, megavitamin therapy, patterning, or treatment of alleged vestibular dysfunction have any benefit above their placebo effects.

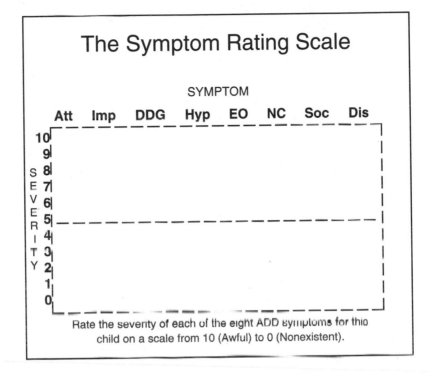

The Symptom Rating Scale

SYMPTOM

| Att | Imp | DDG | Hyp | EO | NC | Soc | Dis |

S
E
V
E
R
I
T
Y

10
9
8
7
6
5
4
3
2
1
0

Rate the severity of each of the eight ADD symptoms for this
child on a scale from 10 (Awful) to 0 (Nonexistent).

10

Behavior Management I:
Ages 2 to 12

M anaging the behavior of an ADD child is quite a challenging
task. In a sense you must be a kind of "professional parent,"
otherwise these kids will tend to have you for lunch on a regular
basis. There are many discipline programs available for children in
general, but some of them are not intended for ADD children.
Attempting to use those that involve only attempts at talking to,
listening to, or negotiating with young ADD kids will drive you
crazy.

In this chapter we will describe some general principles and
some specific methods for managing the behavior of ADD children
between the ages of approximately two to twelve. For parents and
teachers, however, one chapter is too short to learn everything you
need to know to really start doing things not only differently, but
also effectively. For more complete coverage of behavior management principles and techniques, readers are referred to one of our
companion books, *1-2-3 Magic: Training Your Preschoolers and
Preteens to Do What You Want.* Though it can be used with average
as well as problem kids, the "1-2-3" was developed largely on the

basis of lots of experience with ADD children, so the techniques described there are hard-boiled, yet kind and effective.

Thinking ADD: ADD Kids Are Not Little Adults

It's important when dealing with ADD children—and other children as well—to keep your thinking realistic. This means, for example, "thinking ADD." Thinking ADD means *not expecting a regular dose of normal, age-appropriate behavior from your ADD child.*

Realistic thinking also means not getting caught up in the "little adult" assumption. The little adult assumption is the idea that kids are just smaller than we are, but they have hearts of gold and are basically reasonable and unselfish. If your child is not doing his homework, you simply sit him down and explain to him the three golden, irrefutable reasons why he should: 1) he will learn more, 2) it will make you and his teacher happy, and 3) he will grow up to be a responsible and successful person.

The child, naturally, after receiving this wealth of wisdom, responds by saying, "Gee, I never looked at it like that before," and he immediately goes to his room to complete his work. Or imagine your ADD monster is torturing his little sister for the fortieth time since they both got home from school. You ask him how he would feel if someone did that to him all the time. He says, "You know, you're right, I wouldn't like it very much. How insensitive I've been," and he stops—permanently.

This would certainly be nice, but it just doesn't happen. Kids are not little adults. But parents and teachers who believe—or want to believe—this myth are going to rely heavily on words and reasons in dealing with the kids and trying to change their behavior. And words and reasons are going to be miserable failures too much of the time. Sometimes they will have absolutely no impact at all. Other times they will take the parent and child through the Talk-Persuade-Argue-Yell-Hit Syndrome.

Your child is doing something you don't like. You try telling him why he shouldn't do it. He doesn't respond, so you start trying to persuade him to see things your way. When persuasion fails, you start arguing. Arguing leads to a yelling match, and when that fails, you may feel there is nothing left to do but hit. Actually, 90% of spankings and the like are simply parental temper tantrums. Mom or Dad has lost control because they are going out of their mind with frustration and they simply don't have any idea of what else to do.

It is probably true, unfortunately, that ADD kids are more often physically abused than other children are. Part of the reason for this, of course, is that they are often more obnoxious than other children. The other culprit, however, is the "little adult assumption."

How do you get rid of that? You start by changing your thinking about children. This may sound a little strange at first, but instead of thinking of your kids as little adults, think of yourself as a *Wild Animal Trainer*. This does not mean using whips, guns, or chairs. But what a wild animal trainer does, seriously, is choose a method—which is largely nonverbal—and repeat it until the "trainee" does what he wants.

If you have an ADD child, you must become a professional parent, in many ways like the professional wild animal trainer. That means that you must know: 1) what mistakes to avoid, 2) how to categorize the problems you have with your children, and 3) how to handle—or try to handle—each type of problem.

The No Talking, No Emotion Rules

The two biggest mistakes that parents and teachers make in dealing with children are: 1) too much talking, and 2) too much emotion. We just finished discussing why all the talking is bad. It either doesn't work, or it takes you through the Talk-Persuade-Argue-Yell-Hit Syndrome.

Why is too much emotion destructive? It has to do with the fact that when they are little, little kids feel inferior. They feel inferior because they are inferior. They can be cute and nice and lovable, but they are also smaller, less privileged, less intelligent, less skillful, less responsible, and less of just about everything than their parents and the older kids. This bothers them a lot. They don't like it, and they do like to feel they are powerful and capable of making some mark on the world. If a small child can get a big parent or teacher all upset, the upset will make the child feel powerful. It's not that he has no conscience and is going to grow up to be a criminal. It's just that having all that power temporarily rewards— or feels good to—the inferior part of the child.

So a corollary of this is: *if you have a child who is doing something you don't like, get real upset about it on a regular basis and, sure enough, they'll repeat it for you.* There are certainly other discipline systems other than the 1-2-3, but you can ruin any of them for sure by talking too much and getting too excited. These two mistakes, of course, usually go hand in hand, and the emotion involved is usually anger.

Some parents can turn off the talking and the emotional upset like a faucet, and others have to work like dogs to get the job done. Even then, they often have to remind themselves over and over that talking and arguing and yelling and screaming don't really help. These tactics only blow off steam for a few seconds. If a parent finds that they can't shake these habits, some sort of outpatient counseling or psychotherapy is indicated.

Two Categories of Behavior: "Start" and "Stop"

When you are having problems with your kids, they are, in general doing one of two kinds of things. They are either 1) doing something you don't want them to do, or which you want them to stop, or 2) they are not doing something you would like them to start doing. Therefore we call these two kinds of things "Stop" Behavior and "Start" Behavior.

Stop behaviors include the frequent, minor everyday hassles kids get into, such as arguing, whining, fighting, pouting, temper tantrums, disrespect, yelling, and so on. Each thing by itself isn't so bad, but add them all up and by the end of the day a parent may feel like leaving town permanently.

Start behaviors include things like cleaning rooms, homework, practicing obnoxious musical instruments, getting up and out in the morning, bedtime, eating, and so on. Here you want the child to do something that is positive or good.

The reason for distinguishing between these two kinds of behaviors is this: you will generally use different tactics for each category.

• *For STOP BEHAVIOR you will basically use the 1-2-3, or "counting," procedure.*

• *For START BEHAVIOR you will have a choice of six tactics (or combinations of them):*

1. Sloppy PVF
2. Kitchen Timers
3. The Docking System
4. Natural Consequences
5. Charting
6. The 1-2-3 (different version)

When dealing with some trouble with a child, therefore, you will need to first determine if you have a Stop or a Start problem. If you mix up your tactics (e.g., use counting for homework), you will not get as good results or may get no results at all.

The 1-2-3 for Obnoxious Behavior

The 1-2-3 is a simple training procedure for getting children aged 2-12— whether they are ADD or not—to cut out bad behavior. You use it, in other words, to control or eliminate things like arguing, screaming, fighting, teasing, disrespect, etc. You don't use it to get the kids to do the good things, like cleaning rooms, homework, and getting up and out in the morning.

The 1-2-3 is simple. So simple, in fact, that many parents and teachers don't believe that it will work when they first hear about it. However, its effectiveness is supported by the fact that it is used by thousands of parents across the country (many of them parents of ADD kids) as well as by numerous grammar schools, preschools, and day care centers.

Let's say you have a 4 year old who is throwing himself around on the floor, kicking and screaming bloody murder because you refused to give him some potato chips right before dinner. (Typical ADD: bad case of emotional overarousal and low frustration tolerance.) In the past you have not known what to do with these frequent tantrums and nothing has worked.

With the 1-2-3 here's what you do: you look down at the child, hold up your index finger, and say, "That's 1." That's all you're allowed to say.

He doesn't care. He goes on carrying on the same way. After just a few seconds, you hold up two fingers and say, "That's 2." You get the same reaction. So after a few more seconds, you hold up three fingers and say, "That's 3, take 5." That means the child had three chances or warnings to shape up and he blew it—he didn't shape up. So it's off for a "rest period" or time out: five minutes in his room (not in a chair), and then he can come out and you act as if nothing had happened. No lectures or apologies or "Now are you going to be a good boy do you realize what you've been doing to your mother all afternoon why do we have to go through this all the time I'm so sick and tired of your not listening..." Nothing is said. If he misbehaves again, the counting is started again.

Three counts within a 15 to 20 minute period earns a time out. If the child does one thing wrong, however, and then goes 25 minutes with no problem, and then does something else, you start with "That's 1" again.

What if he won't go to his room? With the little ones—say 60 pounds or less—you "escort" them, which may mean follow, drag, or even carry. With older kids, if they don't move at 3, they are then fined 1 cent off their allowance for each minute the time out should have lasted. How long should the time out be? Short and sweet: approximately 1 minute for every year of the child's life (5 year old gets 5 minutes, 10 year old 10 minutes, and so on).

This, of course, sounds too simple. Most parents have heard

of time out procedures, and for some they have worked and for others they haven't. What most parents and teachers don't realize, however, is that the real key to success here has nothing to do with the time out. *The fact of the matter is that the 1-2-3 won't work unless you shut up.* By continuing to talk, you yourself take the responsibility for the child's behavior. You transform the discipline situation into one where they don't really have to respond unless you can give them several good reasons—which they agree with—why good behavior is in order. With ADD kids this, of course, is pure fantasy.

So the disciplinarian is only allowed to say the counts. No other explanations. When the 1-2-3 doesn't work, it's almost always because the adult in charge won't shut up. Here, for example, is one frustrated father's version of the 1-2-3: "That's 1...listen young man, I'm getting sick and tired of this kind of garbage. Do you really want to go to your room... Look at me when I'm talking to you! OK, THAT'S 2! I DON'T KNOW WHY THE HELL YOU CAN'T DO WHAT WE TELL YOU JUST ONCE EVERY TEN YEARS OR SO. THAT'S IT! BEAT IT! OUT OF MY SIGHT—GET UPSTAIRS RIGHT THIS SECOND BEFORE I GET TO YOU! THAT'S 3, DO YOU HEAR ME!"

That's not the 1-2-3. It's simply a parental temper tantrum. It is not effective at all, and it's simply a way of giving a kid a great feeling of perverse power. Just say "That's 1." Be silent and leave the child with the responsibility for their own behavior. If they shape up, fine. If not, "That's 2."

Unfortunately, after reading this your mind may be filled with many more questions about managing obnoxious or "Stop" behavior. It's not the role of this book to answer all of them. Consult *1-2-3 Magic* directly for answers to questions like these:

- What if the child won't stay in his room?
- Won't this make kids hate their rooms?
- How about sibling rivalry?
- What if the child counts you back?
- What do you do in the grocery store?

- How do you handle Testing and Manipulation, such as Badgering, Temper Tantrums, Threats, Martyrdom, Butter Up attempts, etc.?
- How about riding in the car?
- Won't this hurt the child's self-esteem?
- What if my ADD youngster wrecks his room?

Tactics for Start Behavior

Getting children to do what you want them *to do* is another story. Here you can use several different tactics, and you can often be more creative. You can use one tactic, or you can use two or three for the same problem. Your tactics to encourage positive behavior are the following:

1. Sloppy PVF. Sloppy Positive Verbal Feedback, otherwise known as praise or reinforcement, should be dished out on a regular basis. It should be sincere, and usually not too syrupy or overdone. ADD kids don't often take to that kind of thing, since to them it's too discrepant with their self-concept.

2. Kitchen Timers. Kitchen timers are great helps for lots of Start behaviors, such as homework, getting up in the morning, eating, and going to bed. They can also be used to time the time outs themselves. Kids, especially the younger they are, have a natural tendency to want to beat the things.

3. The Docking System. Here the ADD youngster is first given an allowance. Then if the child doesn't do something he's supposed to, like a chore, you do it for him. That's right. But you also charge him for your efforts. Some reasonable fee comes out of his allowance. If he doesn't feed the dog, for example, you take 20 cents out of their $3 per week allowance for each feeding you have to do. No arguing, explaining, or other "little adult" attempts at verbally pounding sense into their heads. Let the money do the talking.

4. Natural Consequences. Here you let the big, bad world teach the child what works and what doesn't. There are times when staying out of some problems is the best thing. Suppose you have a fourth grader who is taking piano lessons for the first time. She is not practicing like she should, however, and then every night is up worrying about her piano teacher being mad at her.

What should you do? Nothing. Some piano teachers are very good at getting uncooperative kids to tickle the ivories on a regular basis.

Or, suppose you have a seventh grader. He's supposed to make his own lunch, with stuff that you buy, and then brown bag it to school. It seems like every day he is yelling at you about how hungry he was at lunch with nothing to eat. What should you do? Relax, and give him some encouragement by saying something like, "I'm sure you'll do better tomorrow."

Another example of a good time to use natural consequences? Wintertime dress. Let them feel a little cold if they're not dressed properly.

5. Charting. Charting involves using something like a calendar which you can put on the refrigerator door, or on the back of the child's bedroom door. You have the days of the week across the top, and down the side each row represents a different task the child is working on, such as cleaning their room, getting to bed, and feeding the dog. If the child completes the task to your satisfaction, you indicate this on the chart with stickers for the little kids (3 to 8) and grades or numbers for the older children.

Reinforcement with charting comes, hopefully, from two things: parental praise (Sloppy PVF) and the inherent satisfaction for doing a good job. These often work well to stimulate a child to do a good job. However, sometimes they don't work. Your kid is just a natural slob and a clean room means nothing to him, or your little girl is ADD and LD, and homework provides very little satisfaction, in spite of your praise.

Here you must go with artificial reinforcers—sometimes referred to as bribery. This is OK, and some kids need to be able to earn something pleasant in order to help them overcome their aversion or indifference to the project. Reinforcers can be part of one's allowance, or special meals, or baseball cards, or staying up later at night occasionally. The best ideas are relatively small things that can be dished out in small pieces and frequently. Try to be creative as possible in coming up with reinforcers—they certainly do not have to always be material.

6. The 1-2-3 (different version). This may seem kind of odd, but the 1-2-3, which was earlier used for Stop behavior, can also be used for Start behavior, but only on one condition: what you want the child to do cannot take over two minutes. So if the child throws their coat on the floor after school, and you ask them to pick it up and they don't, just say, "That's 1." If they get timed out, they go and serve the time, and when they come out, you ask them to pick it up again. If no cooperation, another time out follows. Keep this up until they get the idea.

What if they never get the idea? Just switch to the Docking System. You hang up the coat for them, but you charge for your services. Keep the talking to a minimum, and count whining, arguing, yelling and other forms of hassling.

What can you not use the 1-2-3 for? Obviously, longer projects like homework, eating dinner, getting up and out in the morning, and so on.

You may still have other unanswered questions about the 1-2-3 program, and we don't have time to cover all of them here (see "For More Information" at the back of this book). Here are some of the others that are covered in the *1-2-3 Magic* Video and Book:

1. The child has a tantrum and is timed out. What if the time out is over in five minutes, but the tantrum isn't?
2. What do you do in the car on *really long* vacations?
3. What about whining and pouting—can't they be ignored?
4. What do you do if you're on the phone?

It may seem like an endless list, but it can be managed.

11

Behavior Management II: Adolescents

In dealing with adolescents in general, your overall philosophy should be to gradually stay out of their problems more and more unless it is necessary for you to get involved. The kids are at the point in their lives where they are supposed to be handling more things on their own, and inappropriate attempts at direction from you can cause useless irritation and conflict. Unlike their parents, teens are into dreaming about their futures, struggling to be independent, and identifying more with peers than with their family.

With ADD adolescents this "letting go" is harder for parents because the past has often been so difficult. How do you let go of a child who never seems to do anything right? On the other hand, parents don't want the kids living with them forever, so they have to consider pulling back at some point. When we discuss the Four Steps that parents can use in dealing with their youngsters in the thirteen to eighteen year old range, you may find as a parent that you are using strategies for your ADD teen that are more geared for adolescents about two years younger. This is not unreasonable as long as you continue to try to let go more and more, and don't continue treating your hyperactive offspring as if they were seven years old.

As we did in Chapter 10, in this chapter we will describe some general principles and some specific methods for managing the behavior of ADD adolescents. Again, however, one chapter will be too short to allow anyone to learn all they need to know to manage (*and not manage*) ADD teens effectively without going insane. For more complete coverage, readers are referred to another of our companion books, *Surviving Your Adolescents*, which was also developed largely on the basis of experience with ADD children (see "For More Information").

General Principles

Your state of mind. Make sure you're in good enough shape to try to handle a problem with a teenager, otherwise you're likely to do more harm than good with what is sometimes called "displacement," or emotional dumping. If you are old enough to have a teen, you are old enough to be at midlife yourself, a time which brings many problems of its own for adults. Trying to manage any ADD child when you are strung out with serious personal problems can be a great formula for disaster, so don't kid yourself.

Perhaps a long hard look at your job, your health, or your marriage is in order. Self-help books or groups can also be useful in getting your act together, but if these don't work, getting yourself into some kind of counseling may be necessary.

What sort of adolescent do you have? Being objective about one's own offspring is very difficult, especially when Attention Deficit Disorder has played a large role over the years in helping to shape your opinion. One of the problems with objectivity here is the fact that these kids can be so obnoxious so much of the time. It is very hard to think of someone as competent if they are constantly irritating you. Yet there seems to be a basic rule of psychology which says that most people—children and adults—show their worst behavior at home. That may be the opposite of the way we'd all like it, but it is all too often the case for both kids and parents.

What this can mean to parents of ADD teens is that their children may actually perform the basic tasks of their life a lot better than you think, because you never get a chance to see it directly. What you do see is their irritability, petty sibling rivalry, anger at your direction, and sloppy rooms.

This does not inspire confidence, but it's possible that you are not being totally objective. Therefore it is helpful to take a long, slow, calm look at how the child is doing as far as several things go: home, social life, school, work (if applicable), and general self-esteem. Be careful. Though you may not think of your adolescent as anywhere near competent, are they really the disaster area that you usually imagine them to be? Consider their strengths as well as their weaknesses. In general, the better your child is doing, the less you need to be involved. As you will see later, you will be able to stay more with less intrusive methods.

Your relationship with your ADD teen. Take a long hard look at how well you and this child get along. Consider three things. First of all, how well do you talk with each other, including how often you enjoy just "shooting the breeze" as well as how good you are at solving problems together? Second, consider how much time you spend having fun with one another. This certainly seems to get harder the older the kids get. Finally, how much do you just plain *like* (not love) each other? Be honest. Think of liking as something like finding the other person's presence pleasant most of the time.

If your relationship is fairly good, then you are in a position to intervene or assist your teen when there is a need to do this. If, however, you think your relationship is pretty bad, you have a problem, because you may be the last person on earth who should try to "help." What are your choices? First of all, perhaps you should shut up and let your spouse handle things. (If there is no spouse or if they also have a rotten relationship with the child, you may wind up considering professional counseling.) Second, in any case you need to avoid the Four Cardinal Sins—which we'll discuss in a moment—like the plague. If you don't or can't avoid these, it may be that you are really more out to get your kid than you are out to help them.

Third, perhaps you could consider trying to improve your relationship with the adolescent. This is extremely hard when the relationship has been difficult for many years, and in many situations it is simply impossible. But if you think it might help, there are five "tactics" to consider:

1. Avoiding the Four Cardinal Sins
2. Active, sympathetic listening to what the youngster is saying to you, even if you don't agree or like what you are hearing
3. Talking about yourself (interesting things, not lessons)
4. Shared activities that are fun for both of you (the best bet is probably seeing a movie and then getting something to eat)
5. Realistic, consistent, genuine praise or other kinds of positive reinforcement

These things are discussed in more detail in ***Surviving Your Adolescents***. They require a good deal of commitment and patience on a parent's part and—perhaps above all—the right attitude: the attitude of really trying to get along better, rather than being filled with righteous indignation whenever the adolescent frustrates you with his usual, absurd, ADD behavior.

How serious is the problem? With less serious difficulties, you should be sticking more with the less intrusive alternatives. *Keep in mind that your level of aggravation about a problem is not always the measure of the real seriousness of the problem.* Examples? Earrings on males, jeans with holes.

Your teens, in other words, already have their MBAs! These are the Minor But Aggravating things that they do—things which are irritating to you, but not indications that the kid is in deep psychological trouble. These include problems such as messy rooms, clothes, use of the phone, chores, grammar, and so on. If you have an ADD teen and you are spending a lot of time arguing, lecturing, or complaining about matters such as these, you are missing the boat. You're not likely to change the status quo much at this point anyway, and you probably have other things to worry about that are more important, such as grades, the child's lack of friends, or your difficult relationship with them.

Realistic expectations. If your child has hit the 13 to 18 year old bracket, you're not likely to revolutionize them. Your job of parenting is about 60 to 80% over. With ADD kids this is scary, but be patient and don't slip into ridiculous maneuvers (such as the Four Cardinal Sins). Watch out for the crash course routine and keep your mouth shut unless it's really necessary—absolutely and positively—to say something.

After giving careful consideration to the issues listed above, you are now ready to 1) cut the Four Cardinal Sins out of your behavioral repertoire, and 2) decide which of the Four Steps might be appropriate for the kinds of things you are worried about regarding your son or daughter.

The Four Cardinal Sins

These parental tactics are extremely destructive. Actually, they really don't deserve the label of "tactics," because they are really only primitive, impulsive, and emotional responses that occur without much thought. Doing them on a regular basis means sure death to any relationship with a child. These diabolical maneuvers include:

1. Spontaneous discussions about problems. It's almost impossible to bring up a subject on the spur of the moment with a kid and expect to get anywhere. Spontaneous discussions will almost always increase irritability and decrease cooperation. Believe it or not, you need to make an appointment with the ADD adolescent to discuss important, problematic issues. Take them out to dinner if necessary.

2. Nagging. Nagging never works well and it makes kids

hate you. Nagging could be defined as a set of repetitive, often hostile, verbal reminders from person A, who wants to see something accomplished, to person B, who doesn't share person A's enthusiasm for the project. Behind nagging is the parental delusion that the answer to cooperation lies in repetition.

The antidote to nagging? If the problem is in the MBA category, one answer is obvious. Bite your tongue. If it's absolutely essential to talk, make an appointment.

3. Insight transplants. Otherwise known as lectures, this sin is based upon another bit of wishful thinking on the parent's part. The idea is that Mom or Dad takes one of their wonderful insights about life and sends it through the air waves. It then enters the teen's ears and proceeds to the brain, where it takes root, flowers, and subsequently produces new and more productive behavior.

While on the receiving end of a lecture, kids often think of just one thing: how can I get out of here as soon as possible? Parents sometimes need to open their eyes, look at the youngster's face, and ask themselves how many times they've said the same thing before without much effect. It's not that the ideas in Father's Famous Lecture Series are bad or anything. It's just that lectures also produce much aggravation and little change.

4. Arguing. Arguing with ADD teenagers is one of the things that parents get most fed up with, and the arguments can be pretty near endless when both people insist on having the last word. You certainly are not going to simply shut up and let the child do whatever they want, but it's rare for any adolescent to be argued into genuine submission.

The solution. First, don't argue about MBAs. Second, as with the other sins, make an appointment if something must be discussed. Third, say what you have to succinctly, then clam up or leave. If the teenager then deliberately does something wrong, you will discipline them using some version of Step 4, Taking Charge. Trying to physically or verbally tackle them in order to prevent their doing something you don't like is something that you certainly aren't going to be able to do very long.

We'll talk more about how not to argue a bit later.

The Four Steps

Now that you know something about what not to do, let's consider what to do when there is a problem. The Four Steps—or four alternatives—you can consider using in dealing with your adolescent's problems vary in their level of intrusiveness. From least intrusive to most involved, they are:

> **Step 1: Doing Nothing**
> **Step 2: Consulting**
> **Step 3: Negotiating**
> **Step 4: Taking Charge**

Step 1: Doing Nothing. Believe it or not, there are several ways of doing nothing. If you are having a very difficult time with your own life due to health, depression, marital problems, aging parents, or all of the above and more, you may be in no shape to deal with a troublesome teen. As mentioned before, you can work on your own personal job, health, or marital problems, and, if necessary, keep a watchful eye on what's happening with your child.

You can also do nothing by using the "Grin and Bear It" approach. Before intervening, try more aggressively to "let go." Actually, you really don't need to grin. Unfortunately, however, there are many times when an adolescent can be doing something that irritates the daylights out of you, but you still should not get too involved in it. Perhaps you don't like the way they talk to one of their friends, or they always study with the radio on. Maybe they're eating junk food after school and you think they should have fruit.

Step 2: Consulting. A consultant is a person who is hired to give advice, but with a condition. The receiver of the advice has the right to reject it. If you are going to use Step 2 with your teen, you are not using power and the child has the right to reject your advice.

Unlike most consultants, however, you probably weren't hired for the job. If you are going to give your son or daughter some friendly counsel, remember that it is your idea to do this and not theirs. Keep in mind, once again, that spontaneity can be dangerous. Unwanted advice is a problem by itself, but when the unasked for wisdom comes out of the blue, things are doubly rough. Also, try written rather than verbal requests sometimes; the sound of your voice can be very irritating, especially when repeated "consults" turn into simple nagging. Finally, remember that advice—though good—is cheap and not often followed.

Step 3: Negotiating. "We've got a problem here and sometime I'd like to talk it over with you," might be the beginning of an attempt at negotiation. What you are doing here is recognizing that the ADD child is older now, and that your son or daughter should have some say about many of the things that they do. Negotiating is also a statement that you feel it is important that you be involved, because you think the problem is serious or perhaps because it affects other family members in addition to just the one adolescent. But you are saying that—up to a point—you are willing to bargain or make a deal.

Although Negotiating doesn't have to be anything horribly fancy, it is critical that certain minimal guidelines be followed:

1. Agree to negotiate.
2. Pick a good time and place (a ride in the car is a good idea!).
3. Define the problem.
4. Make a deal or bargain you both can live with.
5. Experiment with the "deal," and change it if necessary.

Step 4: Taking Charge. For too many families there are times when no amount of consulting or talking is going to do any good. Things have gone too far, problems have gotten too serious, and relationships have been too bad for too long. When things get to this point, it is time for Mom and/or Dad to draw the line. This obviously isn't easy to do, and for most parents the idea of trying to tell their adolescents what to do—or to try to force them to do it—

brings up images of ferocious retaliation.

When a problem is serious enough (drugs) or interferes directly with your life (loud music), you have a definite right to Take Charge and become the director of a solution. If the child is uncooperative, the relationship is poor, and all other steps haven't worked, the use of power is legitimate—provided that this use is not just a camouflaged attempt at waging War.

Here's a brief summary of the Major/Minor System:

1) All previous Steps have failed.
2) The problem is important.
3) If both parents are living at home, sit down with spouse, define the problem precisely, decide how to take a stand, and prepare for testing.
4) Give *written* warning.
5) Reinforce compliance.
6) If no compliance, implement consequences.
7) Stick to it with no arguing.

A three category (Major/Medium/Minor) system might look something like this:

Major: offenses could include: out all night, physical violence, drinking and driving, party without permission at home with no parents. Consequences for Major offenses could include: $25 fine, no TV 1 month, no phone or car 1 month, 10 hour chore or project around the house, or grounding for 2 weeks (can't leave house except for work or school).

Medium: offenses might be behavioral trouble at school, smoking (13-15 year olds), swearing using the "F" word, friends at home without permission. Consequences for Medium offenses could include: $10 fine, no TV 2 weeks, no phone 2 weeks, 4 hour chore, or 1 week grounding.

Minor: offenses might include leaving your tools out, swearing using the "S" word, leaving house unlocked. Consequences possible: $1-2 fine, no TV 3 days, no phone 3 days, or 4 day grounding. When the misbehavior occurs, you then institute the consequence without yelling, lecturing, or arguing.

A guaranteed law of adolescent psychology is this: repeatedly engaging in one or more of the Four Cardinal Sins will always obliterate the effectiveness of any consequence or punishment.

Taking Charge with an adolescent can also involve getting the kids into professional counseling, hospitalization, or even kicking them out of the house.

How Not to Argue

We hope the suggestions made so far will be helpful, but just in case they seem a bit too general, we'll end up with some down -and-dirty specifics about how to avoid perhaps the most common of the Four Cardinal Sins, arguing. One of the hardest things to do with ADD teens is to stop arguing. Arguing is a useless, provocative, depressing, addictive, irritating behavior that too often seems to be an irresistible and inevitable part of family life. How can you possibly stop doing it?

This is obviously easier said than done, but parents who learn the art of not arguing can go a long way toward having a much more peaceful home. If you are going to deal with this problem more effectively with your ADD adolescent, you first need to Realize Several Things, then you need to know Exactly What To Do.

Realize Several Things:

1. Arguing doesn't work. No teenager in the history of mankind has ever been argued into sincerely saying, "Gee, Dad, after your brilliant (though somewhat long) explanation of the problem, I now see your point and will comply immediately."

2. Arguing usually escalates. If you participate in some stupid discussion about something that shouldn't even be talked about, the "discussion" will become verbal war.

3. You control about 50% of the problem. Arguing takes two people. It's very hard to argue with just yourself making all the

noise. Your shutting up can help a lot.

4. Teens love to bait you. They can be clever and sneaky and provocative. Before you know it, you're involved and gabbing your head off. Imagine your adolescent is a fisherman sitting in a boat, dropping a baited hook down into a lake. Imagine you are a fish living in the lake. What kind of fish? A large-mouthed bass. Take the bait and you're dead.

Exactly What To Do:

1. Stop Talking. If you control 50% of most arguments, and arguments are purposeless, you should obviously... SHUT UP! This advice, interestingly enough, is so simple that it sounds almost stupid. The real problem, though, is that just shutting up certainly doesn't end the problem right away, because few ADD teens are going to shut up along with you, so...

2. You need to know how to handle their next move. It will be one of the six types of testing and manipulation: Badgering, Intimidation, Threat, Martyrdom, Butter Up (unlikely), and/or Physical. Without actually having to say it, your message to the adolescent will basically be: "I'm out of this stupid discussion. The next move is yours. If you leave me alone, fine. If you hassle me, I'm ready." Ready, though, does not mean more stupid talking.

Of course it's still not that simple, so here's the usual, endless series of questions.

Question 1. What if they keep talking? (Badgering)

Answer: Who's controlling your mouth, them or you? Keep quiet.

Question 2. What if I keep quiet, and they just stand there yelling at me and they won't shut up? (Badgering)

Answer: You have two choices. Go about your business and do your best to pay no attention. Try not to smirk or act superior; you'll only make them worse. If that doesn't work, leave. Go out in the car, go to the bathroom, go for a walk. Anything.

Question 3. What if they follow me all around the house yelling at me? (Intimidation, Physical)

Answer: You have two choices. Go about your business and do your best to pay as little attention as possible. If that doesn't work, just sit down—with them right on top of you—and try to look at a magazine. If they grab the magazine out of your hands, just sit and stare at them. Don't say anything! If you feel like crying, cry. But don't talk.

Question 4. What if they have the last word?

Answer: Are you kidding? Words are cheap. Let them have it.

Question 5. What if they threaten to run away or to break something? (Threat)

Answer: If they threaten to run away, don't say anything. If they do leave (Physical), don't try to stop them. If they're not back when they're supposed to be, there will be consequences for violating their hours. If they're gone into the night, call the police. If they break something (Physical) not so valuable (e.g., a broom), they will have to pay for it later. Don't start talking to them about it. If they start breaking valuable things, call the police.

Question 6. What if they say, "I know it's hard for you to deal with me, but I really appreciate your working so hard at setting limits in order to help me become a responsible adult." (Butter Up)

Answer: What?

Question 7. What if they say I don't love them and never did, or if they say that I never talk to them? (Martyrdom)

Answer: Shut up.

Isn't this fun? No, but you don't have a lot of options. Either keep quiet or pour gasoline on the fire.

12

Medication

The use of medication in the management of Attention Deficit Disorder often provides dramatic assistance to the other parts of the multimodal treatment package. It has frequently been estimated, based upon the extensive research on pharmocological interventions, that medication can be a significant help for 75% or more of the children who are correctly diagnosed ADD. Before beginning an attempt at using drug therapy, however, several things should be discussed with the child, family, and the professionals treating the problem.

1. The attitudes of the child and parents toward the use of medication need to be brought out, clarified, and discussed. Most all parents are concerned—and many are quite worried—about the prospect of their child taking pills. Time should be taken to listen to their concerns and to provide the needed information about things such as the drugs that might be considered, possible benefits, possible side effects, doses, and the procedures used in making adjustments.

These same things should be explained to the child about to

take any medication in words that they can understand. Many kids are quite open-minded about taking medication. Their attitude is something like, "If it will help, why not?" Others—especially older children and teens—may be more resistant. Some may have heard of Ritalin, and they may have negative associations in their minds about it's being a "behavior pill," or a "chill pill," or about it's being used with severely disturbed kids.

Carefully discussing these kinds of concerns with parents and children can go a long way toward increasing long-term compliance with drug treatment. More than once research has indicated that a disturbingly high percentage of parents take their children off medication therapy for the wrong reasons, with the result that too many children (not to mention parents and teachers) suffer unnecessarily.

2. The use of medication in the beginning is only a trial, not a sure thing or a lifetime project. Although the chances of some positive response are very good, not all kids will experience benefits. Some—less than 10%—may encounter side effects which prevent the continued use of a particular drug. Other drugs may then have to be tried. Sometimes finding the right medication and the right dose happens in just a few weeks. Other times, though fortunately less frequently, several different medications have to be tried and the experimentation may go on for several months before the right one—or best one—is found.

How long will a child need to take medication? It's impossible to predict in the beginning. We know some children will need to continue through high school and college. There is also some evidence that after two years of successful drug therapy, about 25% of ADD children can discontinue medication and continue doing well. This kind of determination, though, needs to be done very carefully, for the right reasons, and at the right time.

3. Medication is not a cure. It should not be used by itself; it should be combined with any other needed treatments. Even when drugs do provide significant benefit, they usually provide assistance for only a short period of time. The regular (not slow-release) forms of both Ritalin and Dexedrine, for example, only last about four hours or so. Though certain other drugs can have more long-lasting effects, this means that there will still be regular times in the lives of many children when no medication is available to help. Many parents who have kids successfully taking stimulant meds know how difficult mornings before school and evenings can continue to be!

4. There are contraindications for some medications right off the bat. The presence of a persistently high anxiety level, tics, or psychosis, for example, may rule out the use of any stimulant in a child. Stimulants are often not used—or followed with great caution—in children under six years of age. Certain cardiac problems might militate against using the tricyclic antidepressants. Limited ability of a family to follow through with medication administration, especially with the meds that must be taken consistently, can be a serious drawback. Other families have had a history of drug abuse, either in the children or the parents, so the presence of Schedule II drugs around the house must be considered very carefully.

5. Any child about to take psychotropic medications for Attention Deficit, therefore, should have a physical exam, or should have had a recent one that is relevant to the medications being considered. A baseline blood pressure for example, would be important before Dexedrine or clonidine, and a baseline EKG before using one of the tricyclics.

Several kinds of medications have been found to be useful with Attention Deficit Disorder. Most often used, of course, are the stimulants: Ritalin, Dexedrine, and Cylert. Next in terms of frequency of use come the antidepressants. These include what are known as tricyclic antidepressants, such as Tofranil, Norpramin, and Pamelor, as well as some of the "new generation" antidepressants, such as Wellbutrin and Prozac. Following the antidepressants we have Catapres (clonidine), an antihypertensive medication. The final category of medications, used at times when other conditions coexist with ADD, might be called the "other" category. This list includes drugs such as Tegretol (an anticonvulsant), lithium (a natural salt), and Mellaril (a major tranquilizer).

The Stimulants

Many people find it nonsensical that stimulant medications would be able to calm down a hyperactive child, but this is in fact what often happens. The theory behind this is that the brain and central nervous system of the ADD child—the "governor" of his behavior—is actually understimulated, or lazy. Because this governor is lazy, chaotic behavior results. It is thought that the stimulants in some way stimulate this lazy governor to do his job correctly, with the result that the child is able to be more focused and more organized.

Ritalin. By far the most frequently prescribed drug for ADD is Ritalin (generic name: methylphenidate). This medication is used probably more than all the other drugs put together, and this use is not unjustified. Ritalin has the best track record compared to any of the other available medications except Dexedrine.

Ritalin comes in a 5, 10, and 20 milligram regular form, the effects of which can last generally from three to four hours. After taking the medication, positive effects—if they are going to occur—will show up in approximately thirty to forty-five minutes. The maximum recommended daily intake of Ritalin is 60 mgs.

Ritalin also comes in a 20 mg slow-release (SR) form, which is supposed to last seven or eight hours. For many kids the advantage of this is not having to take a second lunchtime dose during the school day. Unfortunately, although Ritalin SR works fine for some children, it tends to be erratic and should be watched carefully, especially in the beginning. Many kids can't take it because it takes too long to kick in, it fades too quickly, or it just doesn't seem to work at all—even though the regular form of the medication may have worked well. In addition, for small children (under about sixty pounds), 20 mgs is simply too much of a dose.

Also worth watching carefully is the generic form of Ritalin, methylphenidate. Although it is, of course, much cheaper, for many kids it does not produce results that are as good as the brand.

Dexedrine. *Dexedrine (generic name: dextroamphetamine) probably should be used as much as Ritalin, because its track record with regard to benefits and side effects is just as good.* For some reason, though, it is not considered as often as its more popular sister, with the result that many kids kept on Ritalin suffer because they could do better on Dexedrine.

Dexedrine comes in a 5 mg regular form which also lasts about four hours and kicks in about as fast as Ritalin. The maximum recommended per day is 40 milligrams. Milligram for milligram, Dexedrine is about twice as strong as Ritalin (e.g., 10 mg of Ritalin equals 5 mg of Dexedrine). This should be taken into account when switching from one of these medications to the other.

Dexedrine also comes in 5, 10, and 15 mg slow-release forms called "spansules." This form of the drug can last approximately seven to nine hours. Dexedrine SR seems to be much more reliable than Ritalin SR, and should be considered as a possibility much more frequently than it is. Unfortunately, it is occasionally difficult to find the medication in stock at the friendly neighborhood pharmacy, but this problem can usually be solved when the pharmacy knows in advance what the family will need. With the Dexedrine spansules the flexibility of having three different dose sizes is also an important advantage.

Cylert. The third most often used stimulant medication is Cylert (generic: pemoline). Although in studies overall, Cylert is not quite as effective as Dexedrine or Ritalin, it still has an impressive record and should be considered if the other stimulants have not worked, or sometimes in older children where compliance during the day may be a problem.

Cylert is different from the other two stimulants in several respects. First, it comes in weird doses, the smallest pill being 18.75 mgs. Then there is a 37.5 mg tablet and a 75 mg tablet. Cylert is only a slow-release medication, and when it works its effects can last 9-12 hours (some say even longer). This can certainly be an advantage if the medication stays around long enough to help with homework. Cylert may kick in a little more slowly than the other stimulants, and the maximum recommended dose per day is 112.5 mgs. Unlike Ritalin and Dexedrine, Cylert must be taken every day to maintain adequate blood levels. It can also take up to three weeks or so for it to begin working, even if the appropriate dose has been reached. In terms of cross-equivalence, 37.5 mgs of Cylert may be about the equivalent of 20 mgs of Ritalin (or 10 mgs of Dexedrine).

Getting Started with Stimulants: Dexedrine and Ritalin

With most ADD children, the stimulant medications will be tried first, assuming there are no major contraindications. Very conservative doses should be used in the beginning and the child's response should be monitored very closely.

Which drug should you begin with? The answer is *either* Ritalin or Dexedrine. Then after an adequate trial of the first is completed, the other ought to be tried. Too many people think Ritalin is the only game in town, and Dexedrine has been for a while kind of the "forgotten" drug in the treatment of ADD. When a medication trial is indicated for a recently diagnosed ADD child, though, both drugs need to be tried because the overlap in defining who is a nonresponder by any definition (e.g., unimproved behavior or presence of adverse effects) is not great. Unfortunately, there are no predictors of differential drug response, thus necessitating a trial of both. Which drug is chosen first is arbitrary.

Ritalin and Dexedrine, in other words, are definitely the most useful drugs overall in treating ADD. Studies using both drugs have reported positive response rates from 70 to 85%, but there is no clear indication in the literature that one is preferable to the other, either in terms of positive effects or side effects or both. Individual children may respond quite differently to one or the other. Therefore, some recent studies seem to indicate that if careful trials are done with both of these medications with each child, the positive response rate may increase to 90%.

In fairness to the child, consequently, both medications should be tried—in either order—to see which one the ADD youngster does better with. At the completion of the two trials, all the information is reviewed and the period of highest functioning (behavioral, academic, social) and minimal adverse side effects should be identified. The child should then be maintained on that medication and dose.

Although this double initial trial idea with Dexedrine and Ritalin is obviously the best way to go, there is still a good deal of difficulty in getting cooperation with the process from many prescribing physicians, who still lean too heavily on Ritalin alone.

The Stimulant Adjustment (Titration) Process

It still happens too often that stimulant medications are not initially prescribed and adjusted in ways that really make sense. Overdosing, underdosing, and improper adjustment are still all too common. Using Ritalin as an example, let's take a look at a good way of starting, adjusting, and managing medication.

How do you determine the right starting dose? Research seems to indicate that a general rule of thumb for Ritalin is that *about* .5 milligrams per kilogram (2.2 pounds) of bodyweight will be an appropriate therapeutic dose, if the medication works. This is only a very general guideline, of course, because children vary so much in terms of their sensitivity to medications.

What this means, though, is that you can use this formula to guess what might be a helpful dose. Then after you have made your estimate, you start the child out on a slightly lower dose. This gives them a chance to get used to the meds gradually, and it also protects those who might be more sensitive.

One way to calculate the dosage is this. Take the child's weight in pounds and divide it by four. That will give you the total daily amount for both morning and lunch doses added together (but not including any after school "boosters") that you would expect to work. You might expect an 80 pound child, for example to do well with 20 milligrams (80/4) per day, 10 mgs in the morning and 10 mgs at lunchtime.

You would not start the child on a 10-10 regime right away,

however. You would drop down to 5 mgs per dose, to be on the safe side. The 5-5 dose would then be tried for 3 to 5 days. If there are no beneficial effects and no side effects, the dosage would be increased to 10-10. If no effects are noticed in another 3 to 5 days, the dose can be increased again by 5 milligram increments. This continues till one of three things happens: 1) a good therapeutic effect is achieved, 2) side effects occur which can't be tolerated, or 3) the recommended limit of 60 mgs per day is reached.

What if the child is smaller, say 43 pounds? Divide 43 by 4 and you get approximately 10, so you might expect the best dose to be 5 mgs in the morning and 5 at lunch. You still do not want to start right at 5 milligrams with a small child, so the pills should be broken in half, providing doses of 2.5 mgs each. Then you go 3 to 5 days on that dose, and if no benefits or side effects are seen, you increase the dosage by increments of 2.5 milligrams. For children under sixty pounds, 5 milligram jumps in dosage are often too much.

Dexedrine is about twice as strong as Ritalin, milligram for milligram, so Dexedrine doses would be about half what you would use according to the formulas above.

Note several things about the medication titration process described here. First of all, for Ritalin and Dexedrine the trial period for one particular dosage is relatively short, 3 to 5 days. A month is not necessary and wastes time. Second, you do not simply come up with a body weight estimate of the dosage and then sit on it forever. You start lower, and then go upward. Third, frequent and consistent monitoring of the medication's effects is essential, especially in the beginning.

Medication Holidays. Many children with ADD do not take the stimulant medications after school, on weekends, or during summer vacations. Others need to. What determines whether or not a child should take the medication outside of school? Behavioral difficulties, social problems, and special situation demands should be examined.

Many ADD children, when not taking the medication, present behavior which is still much too difficult for parents and others to manage even using the best management methods. It is, therefore, in everyone's best interests if the medication is continued, while keeping a close watch on possible side effects, such as insomnia or appetite suppression at dinnertime. Medication, however, should not be used during these times as a replacement for sound discipline and training.

It's amazing how many people still think stimulant medications are no help with a child's social life, or are "only for school." Very frequently these meds can assist an ADD child tremendously in getting along with others. While it may be true that no medication can "teach" a child anything new, these drugs can help the child calm down, and be less impulsive and pushy. Very often, though not always, the ADD child simply becomes a whole lot less irritating to play with. In children where this occurs, it would seem to be rather unfair to let the kid go out and play during the summer without the help of the medication.

Some ADD kids can get along fairly well outside of school not taking the medication but they may take it periodically for special situations. This PRN—or as needed—use can be a lot of help to everyone, and it may not require a lot of extra dosing. With the approval of the prescribing physician, of course, using the medication for short periods of time to help manage things like Sunday school, long rides in the car, birthday parties, and the annual family picnic may be a very good idea.

Stimulants: Possible Good Effects

Just about anything that can be a symptom of ADD can be helped temporarily by stimulant medication. There is no guarantee, however, since this is a trial and error process and kids react differently, but lots of research shows that the following benefits do occur regularly for many, many children:

- Increase in concentration
- Less impulsivity
- Improved grades
- Less aggressiveness

- Less noisiness
- More cooperation with requests
- Less disruptive in class
- Less hyperactivity and restlessness

Although the child's IQ itself probably does not increase, the child's grades in school will usually improve over time. Oddly enough, though, a number of studies have shown that with prolonged medication therapy scores on standardized achievement tests do not, on the average, improve for ADD kids.

Stimulants: Possible Side Effects

More than 90% of the ADD children who take stimulant medications will not experience side effects which prevent them from continuing drug therapy (provided the medication also works). These negative reactions, in addition, almost always disappear with the discontinuation of the drug and/or a switch to another medication.

The list of unwanted side effects associated with stimulants includes the following:

- Appetite suppression: very common but usually tolerable
- Insomnia: rare when meds are taken earlier in the day
- Headache: can occur in the beginning of therapy, usually goes away
- Stomachache: same as above
- Sadness/irritability: rarer, but may necessitate discontinuation
- Drowsiness: usually a sign that too much medication is being taken
- Increased hyperactivity: fairly rare
- Tics: very rare, discontinuation usually stops the problem

Some parents (less than 20%) report a kind of "backlash" or "rebound" problem with kids taking Ritalin or Dexedrine. What seems to happen is that as the medication is leaving the child's system in the afternoon or evening, the youngster becomes extremely irritable and hard to manage, often much worse than their regular ADD self. This difficult period most often seems to last only about one half hour, but parents have reported that in some kids it seems to go on all evening. In those cases it's hard to tell if this is due to some continuing chemical problem, or if the bad start to the evening itself did irrecoverable damage.

Backlash seems to happen with about 10 or 15% of those kids taking stimulants. There are several ways to try to manage it. Some parents just try to stay out of the kid's way during the dangerous half hour after school. This is not the time to ask them about homework or to demand they clean their room! Sometimes adding a smaller booster dose can help carry the child safely into the evening, and the backlash doesn't seem to repeat later. Other times reducing the last dose in the school day may make some difference. As usual, solving this problem is a trial and error procedure.

Discontinuing Stimulant Medication Therapy

Most ADD children who benefit from stimulant medications will need to continue taking the medication for years, perhaps through high school and college. We no longer believe, obviously, that ADD is something that will be outgrown. Some children will discontinue drug therapy prematurely because their parents saw a misguided news show on TV, or because their grandmother read a disturbing article in a magazine and started giving Mom and Dad some heat about their child's "taking drugs." The total amount of personal, human tragedy caused by such unfortunate decisions is impossible to calculate.

Some children, however, will be able to discontinue meds— for the right reasons—before they are out of school. How this happens we are not sure, since ADD is normally not outgrown or cured by treatment. Perhaps these children are extremely intelligent, or have only marginal cases of ADD, or perhaps, while on the medication, they learned a bunch of new habits that somehow were powerfully reinforced. Whatever the case, some children can stop the meds and still continue to function well.

Many professionals recommend trying a child off stimulant medication every two years or so to see if they can be successful on their own. If you consider doing this, several rules should apply:

1. With Ritalin and Dexedrine, the periods off the medication can be very short: no more than two weeks. Sometimes all you need is two days to tell that things are not working! Don't punish the child and everyone else by keeping them off the meds.

2. Explain to the child what you are doing, and that there is a very good possibility that they will need to continue using the medication.

3. Sometimes "accidental medication holidays" will have already told you that the child is not ready. With many families children have occasionally gone to school after forgetting to take the medication in the morning, and many of these families have been guaranteed of a call from the school because the child's behavior and attention are suddenly so much worse.

4. Never in September! Never do a medication holiday in the beginning of the school year if the child was doing well with medication at the end of the previous year. *This absurd idea is often based on the child's behavior during the summer while off medication, but summertime does not usually require you to sit still and concentrate on boring things.* Let the child start out the new year on his best foot, then consider trying them off in November (not December because of the holiday excitement), when nothing much is going on.

The Antidepressants

The second class of medications used with Attention Deficit Disorder is the antidepressants. This does not necessarily imply that all ADD kids are depressed, though this is not infrequently the case, especially with older kids. It is just that the antidepressants can have some effects that are sometimes helpful with ADD, and they also have a longer duration of action that makes them more attractive sometimes than the shorter acting stimulants.

The tricyclic antidepressants, such as Tofranil (generic: imipramine) or Norpramin (generic: desipramine), may be considered in several different situations. The first situation is **where the stimulants have not been successful or have produced side effects** that could not be tolerated. Be careful here, though, because too often the stimulant trials followed the "Ritalin-to-Cylert-and-out" program—totally ignoring Dexedrine. Or the trial may have been inadequate for some other reason. A difficult ADD child who does not respond to a stimulant presents a vexing problem to himself and others, and many times the antidepressants can help quite a bit.

There is a second type of situation in which antidepressants might be the first medication to be tried. This can occur **when there is a major contraindication for stimulants**, such as the existence of tics in the child or a strong family history of Tourette's Disorder. Antidepressants may also be tried first when there is an ADD child who is also experiencing a good deal of anxiety or depression. These medications, of course, were originally intended to deal with depression, but they can also have a significant effect when it comes to reducing anxiety. When taken before bed, they help many ADD children sleep much better as well.

In a third instance, **antidepressants may help when the stimulants are already being used, but their benefits simply last too short a period of time.** Some children, for example, do well on Dexedrine during the day, but are still holy terrors at night in spite of the best parental efforts at firm management. To cover these evening periods—and perhaps even the difficult mornings—medications like imipramine and desipramine can be helpful in reducing difficult behavior.

Many of the tricyclic antidepressants come in 10, 25, 50, and 100 milligram sizes, as well as larger pills. Adults, when taking them for depression, can usually achieve consistent therapeutic blood levels after three weeks or so by taking the medication only once a day. Some children can do this, but because of their higher metabolism kids may require twice a day dosing, usually morning and before bed. In order to maintain blood levels these drugs should be taken every day, seven days a week. Even though they are not addictive in any way, sudden discontinuation can cause temporary, flu-like symptoms (e.g., headache, nausea).

There seem to be differing opinions as to how long it takes for the antidepressants to kick in after beginning therapy. Many experts forecast that it takes ten to fourteen days before results are seen, but this prediction may be largely based on the data gathered from the treatment of adult depressed patients. Other clinicians have said that they often see results much sooner, and this certainly does seem to happen.

Therapeutic doses with imipramine and desipramine have been found in the ranges between 1 to 5 milligrams/kilogram per day. A seventy-five pound youngster, for example, taking 100 mgs of Tofranil each day would be at approximately 3 mg/kg. Initially, tricyclics were dispensed rather liberally, with higher doses not uncommon. Then it seemed that most physicians were reluctant to exceed the 3 mg/kg point, due to concerns about possible cardiac side effects. The general feeling today is that higher than 3 mg/kg doses are often necessary to achieve a therapeutic blood level, but that any treatment with tricyclics should be accompanied by appropriate cardiac monitoring, such as baseline and follow-up EKGs.

What benefits can you expect? Antidepressants can produce behavioral effects similar to those resulting from stimulant use. With the antidepressants, though, these effects may last longer. Studies have reported the positive effects to include reductions in hyperactivity and aggression. Parents often report that children taking antidepressants are more compliant, less impulsive, and less overemotional. Some of these medications have also helped with things like bedwetting, night terrors, and sleepwalking.

When antidepressants are prescribed for ADD kids who have shown significant amounts of anxiety and/or depression, reductions in these problems can be expected. Often changes in these emotions carries along with it a marked reduction in the child's level of irritability as well as improvements in sleep patterns.

One problem with the antidepressants is that although some

studies have suggested these drugs can help with concentration, especially Norpramin, clinical experience suggests that any attentional benefits are either fairly weak or nonexistent. Whatever improvement in attention that may occur with some kids certainly is not as dramatic as what happens with the stimulants. For this reason, some children will take a stimulant and an antidepressant concurrently. This is normally a reasonably safe procedure, and one must be aware of the fact that the presence of a stimulant in the blood stream may slow down the metabolism of an antidepressant. This somewhat elevates the blood level of the antidepressant, but not usually in a way that becomes dangerous to the child.

Side effects with antidepressants are not usually significant, but they can occur as they can with any medication. They can include dry mouth, increase in blood pressure and pulse, nausea, drowsiness, and slowing of intracardiac conduction. Close monitoring of cardiac function is generally recommended, especially in children taking more than 3 mgs/kg per day.

Other tricyclic antidepressants that have at times been considered for use with Attention Deficit Disorder include Elavil (amitriptyline), Pamelor (nortriptyline), and Anafranil (clomipramine). Two of the "new generation" antidepressants, Wellbutrin and Prozac, have also been used, but not extensively so far with children. In adults these newer drugs are noted for having fewer side effects.

Clonidine

Clonidine (brand: Catapres) is actually a medication used primarily for people with high blood pressure. While this may sound odd—using an antihypertensive for Attention Deficit—it is probably no more strange than using a stimulant or antidepressant. Clonidine has some advantages as well as some disadvantages when compared to Ritalin, by far the most commonly used medication. Stimulants like Ritalin have a short duration of action (3-4 hours for the regular form), and some people feel that children treated with it may suffer from a recurrent oscillation of behavior control—a kind of rollercoaster effect. Some children can experience increased hyperactive behavior in the afternoon or evening as the medication's effect wears off.

This can certainly happen, though most children do not get worse in the evening and "backlash" effects are usually short-lived. The dosage and type of stimulant medication used, of course, should be carefully titrated.

What type of ADD children might be considered candidates for this medication? According to some writers, the optimal clonidine responders are highly aroused ADD children who are very overactive and energetic. Based on experience with hundreds of children taking clonidine, there seems to be a clinical subtype of ADD children who usually have low frustration tolerance and may exhibit signs of conduct disorder, oppositional behavior, aggression, and explosiveness. These children might benefit from this drug, but one should keep in mind the fact that the stimulants are usually better when it comes to helping with selective attention and distractibility.

Clonidine can help reduce this hyperactivity and over-arousal, however. In several studies parents and teachers described the children on clonidine as more cooperative, more willing to complete their homework, and more willing to carry on conversations. Their frustration tolerance also seemed to improve.

As with medication treatment in general, follow-up and careful monitoring is critical. As with some other medications, some physicians feel that the generic (clonidine) is not as effective as the brand medication (Catapres).

The maximal effects of clonidine, if they occur, may not be evident for one to two months. Now that's a slow kick in period! There may be an initial effect of sedation, such as sleepiness, but this usually subsides after a few weeks and the patient remains calm and alert. A gradual maturation may unfold as the child is able to calmly apply his ego strength to the problems of living. Some parents say they're not sure if it's the medication or if the child has simply "grown up some and matured the way he's supposed to."

Doses of clonidine sound extremely low, but remember that you cannot compare milligrams across medications. An average 10 year old may start on as low as .05 mg (1/2 tablet) once a day for three days, gradually building up to 0.2 to 0.3 mgs per day. Clonidine also comes in skin patches, which can be worn on the back and can usually survive showers and sweating. It has also been used along with Ritalin in ADD children with high levels of activity and distractibility who remain inattentive even after their behavior is calmed by clonidine.

Contraindications to using clonidine? Watch out for children who may be depressed or have a history of depression, children who are psychotic or have thought disorders, and kids who might qualify as ADD without hyperactivity. Since clonidine is an antihypertensive, blood pressure is also a concern and should be monitored.

Clonidine is definitely a promising medication. The possibility of a round-the-clock calming effect is very attractive, though it does require three or four doses per day. Slow onset of action and frequent absence of concentrational benefit are drawbacks. Don't jump on any bandwagon before you carefully analyze the needs of *your* child.

Other Drugs

Drugs in our "other" category here include those that are used less frequently with ADD and those that may be used for ADD and comorbid conditions. These drugs include Tegretol, lithium, and Mellaril.

Tegretol (carbamazapine). Tegretol is an anticonvulsant which is primarily used to treat seizures. It has also been shown to be effective with some types of behavioral problems (especially when brain damage is suspected), such as aggressiveness, extreme anger, and mood swings.

Lithium. Lithium is a natural salt that is available in a number of different forms. Its major use is in the treatment of manic depressive—or "bipolar"—disorder. Like Tegretol, it can sometimes be helpful in managing aggression, mood swings, and some kinds of depression. Lithium needs to be monitored very closely, since therapeutic and toxic blood levels are not as far apart as with most other medications.

Mellaril (thioridazine). Mellaril is one of the so-called major tranquilizers, which are often used to treat psychosis. Psychosis can involve things such as severe agitation, visual and auditory hallucinations, and delusions. Mellaril is sometimes used to help treat what might be thought of as "ADD plus," where a child shows symptoms of ADD but may also be extremely aggressive, conduct disordered, or mentally retarded.

Avoiding Medication Mistakes

The use of medication can be one of the most dramatically helpful parts of the multimodal treatment package. In order to maximize its effectiveness, certain errors must be avoided. The most common are the following:

1. Inadequate prior medical histories or physical exams.
2. Not trying any medication at all.
3. Inadequate follow-up, both during the critical initial titration phase as well as long-term.
4. Ambivalence about using drugs. This can give rise to underdosing with a potentially helpful medication, as well as discontinuing any attempt at drug therapy after only one drug has been tried.
5. Underdosing or overdosing due to strict adherence to bodyweight formulas.
6. Overlooking family problems or other comorbid diagnoses.
7. Summertime medication holidays that ruin a child's social life.
8. Medication holidays right when a child returns to school in September.
9. Stopping medication abruptly without talking to one's doctor.

10. Believing that medication cannot be used when the diagnosis is ADD *without* hyperactivity. Many of these children benefit greatly.
11. Discontinuing medication simply because a child has hit midadolescence; people can still benefit from medication at age 18, 30, or 50.

This chapter has provided some valuable basics about medication therapy for ADD. Keep in mind, however, that no alterations should be made in any medication treatment program without the explicit knowledge and direction of one's own physician.

Two Important Points

1. "All ADD children deserve a trial of medication since there is absolutely no way to tell which children will respond and which children will not."

Paul Wender, M.D.

2. Unless there are contraindications for using stimulants, both Ritalin and Dexedrine should be tried with each ADD child, since many children respond to one better than to the other.

Note: More information about medication treatment may be found in the new video (available in March, 1994), *Medication for Attention Deficit Disorder*, by Thomas W. Phelan, Ph.D., and Jonathan Bloomberg, M.D. See page 171.

Working with the School

Patricia Graczyk
School Psychologist

In recent years events have occurred on a number of fronts which will directly and indirectly assist you in communicating and working with your child's school. These include the following:

• The U. S. Department of Education issued a memorandum to all state and local educational agencies which clarified the fact that children with ADD may be eligible for support services through the school under Public Law 101-476, the Individuals with Disabilities Education Act of 1990 (IDEA) or Section 504 of the Vocational Rehabilitation Act of 1973 (commonly referred to as Section 504).

• Several well-written resource manuals for teachers were made available which provide a compilation of school interventions for children with ADD (e.g., the *CH.A.D.D. Educators Manual*).

• More teachers are aware of ADD and the needs of the ADD children in their classrooms.

• Educators have a greater awareness that effective home-school partnerships are necessary to insure that students are successful within school.

Educational Implications of IDEA and Section 504 for ADD Children

Some of you may have already heard of Public Law 94-142, the Education for all Handicapped Children Act of 1975. This important law (and its downward extension, Public Law 99-457) in essence guaranteed that handicapped children were entitled to a free and appropriate public education. PL 94-142 encompassed both special education and related services. It also established guidelines by which the rights of handicapped children were protected. When 94-142 was reauthorized in 1990, it was renamed IDEA.

Both IDEA and its predecessor delineate the kinds of handicapping conditions to which they apply. Categories of handicapping conditions covered under these laws include (among others): learning disabilities, seriously emotionally disturbed, mentally retarded, and "Other health impaired." Shortly after the passage of IDEA, the Department of Education issued a memorandum clarifying that children with ADD may be eligible for services and programs covered by this law if they met the criteria for any of the handicapping categories delineated in it. ADD children found eligible for services and/or programs through IDEA are most frequently served under the categories of "Other health impaired," learning disabilities, or serious emotional disturbance.

Even when ADD children do not qualify for services through IDEA, they may still be eligible for services through Section 504. Section 504 applies to a wider variety of individuals with handicapping conditions. In essence, a student with ADD would be eligible for school adaptations and interventions under Section 504 if it is determined that ADD substantially interfered with a "major life activity," such as learning. Both IDEA and Section 504 require a school district to conduct an evaluation to determine if the student has a handicapping condition which warrants educational interventions. Both laws require that these interventions be implemented in the "least restrictive environment." This assures that the child's educational program differs from the standard educational program only to the extent necessary to meet his/her educational needs in a satisfactory fashion.

If a child is eligible for educational support through IDEA, an Individual Education Program (IEP) will be written, which delineates the difficulties the child is experiencing in school and the steps which will be taken to address those difficulties. If a child is eligible for support through Section 504, an Accommodation Plan will be developed and provide similar information. The parents' role in educational planning for their children with a handicapping condition is stipulated by law. Many references are available explaining both the children's rights and those of their parents.

Guidelines for Effective Home-School Partnerships

There are several obstacles which you, as parents, may face in dealing with school personnel. You may, for example, underestimate or overestimate what school professionals can do. Conversely, school staff may underestimate or overestimate what you, as parents, can do! The most common obstacle voiced by many parents is that they feel intimidated by school personnel. This may be fueled, in part, by the parents' belief that school personnel are the "experts" and that they, as parents, have little to offer in discussing and planning their child's educational program. Some educators may hold this belief themselves and convey it to parents either openly or through the manner in which they treat parents.

What, then, can you as a parent do to insure that your child is provided an appropriate education? First of all, remember that, as parents, you were your child's first teachers. In working with school personnel, present yourself as an active, contributing, and essential participant in the educational decisions which will involve your child. Establish and maintain a working relationship with school personnel based on mutual trust and respect. View your role as that of an equal partner in solving the problems your child may face in school. Continue to educate yourself on the needs of children with ADD (yours, in particular!) so you may take a greater role in the problem-solving process.

Problem-solving is a process in which you, as parents of an ADD child, will probably be engaging with school personnel given that ADD symptoms are typically most evident in school. Therefore, it is important for you to be familiar with the steps involved in the problem-solving sequence. In order to demonstrate how this process may proceed we will take a fairly common problem children with ADD have in school: not completing assignments.

Step 1: Problem identification. You may be thinking to yourself that this is an easy step because we already know what the problem is, i.e., the student is not completing assignments. However, in this step, we need to take the stated problem and define it more specifically. In what class(es) is, say, Jimmy not completing his work? Are all his assignments partially done or just some of them? What kinds of assignments is he more likely to leave incomplete? How often does this happen? All of these are examples of questions which may be asked at this step to help identify the problem as specifically as possible. Once there is a clear understanding of the extent and specific aspects of the problem, you then proceed to the next step.

Step 2: Look at the factors which may be contributing to the problem. Is Jimmy not completing his work because he doesn't understand how to do it? Or is he not using allotted time wisely? Or is the assignment lengthy and he is unable to attend for more than 10 minutes at a time? Or are there too many distractions in his work area?

At this step you would also attempt to look at the extent to which the identified factors may be working together both to cause and to continue this problem.

Step 3: Brainstorm alternative strategies. Brainstorming is a process by which participants in the problem-solving process attempt to generate as many solutions as possible to the problem. All possible solutions are accepted without criticism (and often written down). Once all the possible solutions are generated, you proceed to the next step.

Step 4: Discuss alternative strategies and choose the most effective. At this step, you consider the advantages and disadvantages of each brainstormed solution in a systematic fashion until you agree on the ones which appear to be the most appropriate. At times school personnel will have the primary responsibility for implementing chosen strategies, but at other times it may be you. In our example, if Jimmy is not completing his work because he doesn't have a quiet place at home to study, his parents may be the ones who are responsible to find that quiet spot for him.

It is most important at this step that the individuals who will be implementing the strategies agreed upon by the group are, in fact, in agreement with them. After all, they are the ones who will be expected to do the most work. Don't agree to carry out things at home which place too many demands on your time and energy. Many people aren't aware of the extra demands parents of a child with special needs face. On the other hand, be sensitive to the extra demands that children with ADD may present to their classroom teachers. Assure teachers that you understand that interventions expected of them need to be realistic as well.

Step 5: Specify who will be responsible for what. In Step 4 it is usually apparent who will have the primary responsibility in implementing the strategies agreed upon. However, there may be other tasks which need to be done in order to implement the intervention. These other tasks should all be delineated and assigned to insure that the chosen intervention doesn't "fall between the cracks."

Step 6: Initiate the intervention.

Step 7: Evaluate the effectiveness of the intervention. This can be done on both a very informal or more formal basis. A less formal basis may involve minor changes in the planned intervention which "works out the kinks" which may not have been considered at the problem-solving conference. More formal evaluations may include progress review conferences among two or more of the problem-solving team. The purpose of these conferences would be to review what has been done and how successful it has been. The way in which the effectiveness of the intervention will be evaluated should be discussed at Step 5. The formality of the evaluation should be determined by the problem and its severity.

It is suggested that you use this information as a general framework in which to work with teachers and other school personnel when dealing with the difficulties your child may face in school.

When Your Child Is Being Evaluated for ADD

By the time your child is diagnosed as having ADD, you may have already been actively involved with your child's teacher and other school personnel. Since ADD symptoms are typically most apparent within a school environment, it may even be the case that school personnel were the first to share with you the possibility that your child has ADD.

Some parents prefer to conceal the fact that their child is being evaluated for ADD from school personnel as these parents believe it is a family matter and not one of which the school should be informed. In fact, such a decision can actually interfere with the accurate diagnosis of ADD since school functioning is a major component of the assessment process. Typically the person doing the evaluation will request a verbal or written report from the child's classroom teacher(s). As part of the evaluation, teachers are often asked to complete behavior rating scales specifically designed to provide information regarding school difficulties most often encountered by children with ADD. Most teachers are quite willing to provide such information, and these behavior rating scales are often useful later during follow-up to see how well things are changing.

Once a Diagnosis Is Made

Once a diagnosis of ADD is made, it is helpful to alert the school of this fact. If a trial of medication is being considered, *information from the classroom teacher is usually crucial* in arriving at an optimal dosage.

It is suggested that you provide the school with a report from your doctor stipulating that a diagnosis of ADD has been made. In that report doctors sometimes choose to include recommendations they believe would facilitate your child's school progress. It's best to give this report to the school principal (or, for older students, your child's guidance counselor) with a request that it be shared with appropriate school personnel, especially classroom teachers.

Depending on the severity of your child's needs, they may be eligible for a variety of educational interventions. For example, "support" personnel may become involved in educational planning for your child, although some may have been involved prior to diagnosis. Support personnel include school psychologists, counselors, resource teachers, and social workers. Oftentimes these staff members have extensive knowledge of the needs of ADD children and can serve as powerful resources to you, your child, and your child's teachers in meeting your child's educational needs. Support personnel may be involved in the following ways: provide you with information regarding home management techniques, local parent groups, or community activities available for children with ADD; help the classroom teacher implement an effective classroom management program or provide instruction more in line with your child's needs; work with children to improve their social skills; and provide counseling for children experiencing low self-esteem. Children with more serious needs can receive specialized programming for 50% or more of their school day, if necessary.

According to the Professional Group for ADD and Related Disorders, 1/2 the children with ADD can have their educational needs met through modifications in the regular classroom. Of the children with ADD who do require special education, 85% are able to be maintained in the regular classroom for a significant proportion of their school day.

Approximately 30-50% of children diagnosed as having ADD also experience other difficulties such as learning disabilities, poor eye-hand coordination, and low self-esteem. Contingent on the existence and degree to which these other problems are present, your child may be eligible for additional evaluations and services as well.

All public schools are required by law to provide services to students with identified handicaps. Furthermore, the schools must have written policies explaining the procedures by which students are identified and served through these programs.

Transitions from One School Year to the Next

Although school personnel also want to see students start a new school year "on the right foot," there are steps you as a parent can take to facilitate this. Just don't wait until the beginning of a new school year to do them!

Toward the end of the current school year request a progress review and planning meeting with your child's current classroom teacher(s), the principal or guidance counselor, and other support staff who may have been involved in planning and implementing services for your child. At this meeting your child's progress should be reviewed (including what worked and what didn't). Both you and the staff should project what your child will need in order to be successful in the following year.

This may include: hand-selecting a classroom teacher (when there are more than one class of a given grade) or a homeroom teacher, a behavior management program, preferential seating, a peer buddy, a daily assignment sheet, arranging a meeting with the receiving teacher(s) early in the year, and additional services outside the classroom (e.g., academic support, individual or family counseling).

Once your child's new teacher (or homeroom teacher) has been named, make an appointment early in the year to establish a working relationship with him or her. Offer to provide them with information regarding your child's unique needs and a general reference of classroom strategies to use for children with ADD. *Be sure to let them know what specific tactics have worked well with your youngster in the past.* Assure them that you are willing to work with them in meeting the needs of your child and acknowledge the challenge that a child with ADD can present to a classroom teacher.

Whenever meetings are scheduled to discuss your child's educational needs, make every effort to be present and actively participate in them. It's helpful to request that summary reports of such meetings be written and distributed to all participants. Such summaries provide a record of the issues discussed and decisions made. They also help insure that recommended follow-ups are implemented.

As mentioned earlier, more educators are sensitive to the needs of the child with ADD than there were even a few years ago. Although major gains have been made in the area of home-school collaboration, there may still be times when you and school personnel do not agree as to the way to provide your child with a satisfactory educational experience. When you have depleted all cooperative avenues, then you may need to utilize the services of a parent advocate or exercise your due process options. All states have parent advocacy groups. Your local library should be able to provide you with information about them.

As each school year comes around, your children will face new teachers and new challenges. You, as parents, will be the one consistent factor providing continuity to your children's educational program. Be active and confident in your partnership with the school. You have knowledge, experience, and concern for your children which are both unique and important to consider in order to help them be successful in school.

14

Classroom Management

The statistics about ADD suggest that there should be approximately one ADD child in each classroom of twenty to twenty-five children. In some years, of course, a teacher might get lucky and have none. At other times the law of averages may betray them, and they may have more than their share. Even when there is only one, however, the ADD child is very likely to take up a disproportionate amount of the teacher's time and effort.

The suggestions in this chapter are designed to keep that time and effort as manageable as possible, while still providing the necessary direction and support for the ADD youngster. Teachers dealing with ADD kids basically need to master several things:

1. Thinking ADD
2. Crisp behavior management/discipline
3. Prevention of academic and behavioral problems
4. Encouraging the child's best work
5. Dealing with the child's parent(s)
6. Experimental and pragmatic thinking

7. Awareness of some basic medication facts

Mastering these strategies can make the difference between a year of disaster or a reasonably pleasant—or at least tolerable—school year.

1. Thinking ADD

As mentioned earlier, a teacher should not expect normal behavior from a handicapped child. The problem with ADD is the handicap is of the "hidden" variety. The child looks normal, so why can't he behave normally?

This should not be treated as a rhetorical question, i.e., one that is not really a question, but rather a statement of extreme frustration. The answer to it as a legitimate question is: the child can't behave normally because he has ADD, and he can't turn off the ADD at will. Therefore I'd better take a new and different look at this kid.

The best way to do this is by using the Symptom Rating Scale described earlier (see page 85). In the beginning of the year, the teacher can, after a few weeks, do his or her own rating of the extent to which the child shows each of the eight ADD symptoms. A better idea is to do this and then compare it with the parents' own versions and discuss the results with the parents. This exercise helps the teacher be more realistic about what to expect from this boy or girl.

Thinking ADD and using the SRS hopes to accomplish several things. First of all, it gives the teacher a down to earth idea of what the child's behavioral repertoire is. Second, it clarifies for the teacher that the problem is ADD, not a lousy parent or a kid who's out to get them. The problem behavior is also not caused primarily by faults in their teaching strategies. Third, thinking ADD reduces anger because it makes expectations more realistic. Anger is always aggravated the greater the discrepancy between what you expect and what you get.

2. Crisp Behavior Management

How do you handle one ADD youngster and twenty-four non-ADD kids without any big hassles? With great difficulty. The first task here is to divide the children's problem activities into two types: A) Disruptive misbehavior, such as throwing spitballs or blurting out jokes, and B) Nondisruptive, ADD-type behavior such as getting distracted or being restless.

For the disruptive misbehavior, the "1-2-3" method should be used (see Chapter 10). Two verbal warnings, if necessary, then a brief time out (or other consequence) in a predetermined area. Goofing around or other violations of time out may result in immediate withdrawal of an imminent privilege, such as recess or lunch, involvement of someone like a principal, and/or a notification of parents. In using the 1-2-3 properly, of course, the teacher should avoid all excess talking and should remain as calm as possible.

For problems like restlessness or distractibility, other tactics are used that do not involve punishment. Restlessness can sometimes be reduced by one of the prevention tactics (see Legitimate Movement). Or restlessness and off-focus time may be signalled by the teacher to the child. Many teachers prefer a "secret signal" here—one that is, hopefully, known only to the teacher and the child. This is an attempt to not embarrass the youngster and also to engage them in a kind of mutual problem-solving game. When the ADD child is off daydreaming, for example, the teacher gets in a position to be seen and produces the signal—tugging on her ear, scratching her forehead, tapping her elbow with her finger, or whatever she and the child earlier agreed upon. A simple hand on the shoulder can also work quite well.

3. Prevention

Several tactics can go a long way toward preventing problems before they occur. These include the following:

Legitimate movement. Allowing the child brief periods of time to move around is often a real blessing for everyone. These can include going to the bathroom (though not 19 times a day!), sharpening a pencil, stretching, and special trips for the teacher down to the principal's office. Sometimes these can be used as rewards, but this shouldn't be done if the child is never able to earn any.

Desk placement. The desk of the ADD child should be up in front of the room, close to the teacher. This more closely imitates the kind of one-on-one situation where these kids perform better, and it makes it easier for the teacher to monitor the more difficult child's progress. If the child is facing toward the front of the room, it also minimizes distractions, i.e., all the visual and associated auditory stimuli that a child can see if they are seated in the back.

Be careful with cooperative education or team learning. Many ADD kids don't do well when they are asked to work in small groups. Close desk placement sometimes means to them nothing more than three other kids within kicking distance. It can also mean three other, very close verbal and auditory distractors. Some teachers, however, have said that their ADD kids can handle it OK. Another time to gently experiment.

Maximize the child's strengths. Find out what this kid is good at, whether it's math or reading, or simply loving to do errands. Try to give them ample opportunities to engage in their strong suits and then verbally recognize and reinforce their efforts.

Structure helps. Doing things at the same time and in the same place for the most part will help the ADD child focus. Change tends to disrupt their thinking.

4. Encouraging the Best Work

Getting ready. Try to allow nothing on the desktop that is not part of the task at hand. Divide work into small, manageable units (e.g., start with half of an 8.5x11 sheet rather than the whole thing).

Giving directions. Establish eye contact before giving instructions. Use the child's name, if necessary, to keep them with you as you speak. Keep directions as short as possible. Use multiple modes, such as visual and auditory, in presenting instructions or new material.

Attention checks. Sometimes it is helpful to see if the child has really understood what you have said. Some kids become adept at looking you right in the eye while they are paying absolutely no attention! If possible, ask the child in a non-accusing manner what is supposed to be done.

Doing the work. Frequent checks to insure the work is being done are often helpful (there are only twenty-four other kids to check on, right?), since many ADD kids start out with a bang and then fizzle out. If the child is off task, secret signals can be used to bring them back. These kids do best with frequent verbal or physical reinforcement. So do other children, of course, but Attention Deficit students fall apart much faster when reinforcement is not available.

After the work is done. ADD kids often lose it! Help them file work in an orderly, consistent manner. Color-coded notebooks help. Assignment sheets or notebooks for unfinished work should be filled out and checked by the teacher. Even though they may be in seventh grade, too many hyperactive children are simply unable to do this.

5. Dealing with Parents

Maintaining a good and consistent relationship with the child's parents is very important—and often very difficult, and it becomes more and more important the more trouble the child is having. It is very hard to discuss serious, emotionally loaded issues with strangers. Therefore, if a child is coming into a new class and a new teacher, and he has still been showing considerable problems, teacher or parents should meet before the year starts.

Teachers need to remind themselves that these parents probably did not cause their child's bad behavior by the way they raised him. Mothers of ADD kids, in addition, are usually the ones the teachers talk to more often, and many of these mothers will come across as angry, blaming, depressed, or hysterical. Many teachers' reaction to this is something like, "Heck, lady, if I had a mother like you, I'd be hyperactive myself!" Try to keep in mind that this temperamental parental behavior may reflect the exact opposite: the long-term effects of this child on this mother.

Parents need to remember that the teacher has 24 other kids in the class in addition to their child. They must also give the teacher credit for having the same negative emotional reactions to their child that they themselves have at home, instead of somehow expecting the teacher to have semi-infinite patience.

6. Experimental Thinking

There are quite a few recommendations above for managing the ADD child in the classroom. It would be virtually impossible for any teacher to apply all of these to any one ADD child, unless by some miracle that youngster were the only one in the class. It also will be true that not all techniques will work equally well with all ADD children. A teacher, therefore, should take an experimental and pragmatic attitude toward the recommendations, trying to find the ones that do the most good and that are realistic in terms of the teacher's time, energy, and skill.

This can be accomplished in the following way. Before trying anything specific, the teacher looks at the list (and searches her own experience), and identifies tactics that she thinks would be useful. The teacher then sits down with the parents and asks them what strategies have worked most successfully in the past with their child.

When certain techniques have been agreed upon, these will be the ones tried out initially during the year. If they work, fine. If they don't, there's no sense in beating a dead horse—something else should be tried.

ADD kids are notoriously "teacher sensitive," and the person who is in charge of their classroom can have wonderful—or devastating—effects on what kind of year they have.

7. Awareness of Some Medication Basics

Many teachers say, with good reason, that they are not physicians, do not prescribe the medication the child takes, and feel uncomfortable getting involved in this area. This is certainly understandable, but unfortunately this line of reasoning has to be modified because of two obvious facts. First of all, lots of ADD kids are lousy historians; they have great difficulty accurately describing their past experiences, including their positive or negative responses to medications. Second, because of the short duration of action of the medications (Ritalin, Dexedrine) that are most often used for ADD, any possible changes due to the meds are sometimes seen only during the school day.

What this means is that most of the time *the only reliable observer of positive and negative drug effects who is around while the drugs are active is the teacher.* Therefore teachers' observations are extremely critical, partly because they are the only ones available. Teachers, consequently, need to know some basics about the different medications and how they work. It is very important for them to have a general idea of what positive effects might be expected from something like Dexedrine, for example, and they also need to know what some of the possible side effects might be (see Chapter 12).

Teachers certainly don't have to prescribe meds themselves, but they can pass on critical information to parents or directly to the prescribing doctors themselves. In doing so, of course, they can help the ADD child immeasurably, and they can also make their life a lot easier.

Part IV:

ADD in Adults

15

A Lifelong Proposition

For a long time it was believed that Attention Deficit Disorder would be outgrown by the time a person was an adolescent. This idea probably came from the general observation that most hyperactive children seemed to calm down somewhat as they got older. Since the most obvious symptom of the disorder—moving around a lot—lessened, people tended to assume that the rest of the problem was gone too.

Not only is this not the case, but many ADD adults (about 60%) continue to have their ADD symptoms *and also* suffer from added problems that arose from "growing up ADD." Among the more prominent of these "extras" are low self-esteem, depression, and major interpersonal difficulties. That is also why the term, "comorbidity," is often used in describing ADD adults—they often can carry more than one diagnosis.

Paradoxically, for the therapists trying to treat them, Attention Deficit adults can be among the most rewarding as well as the most frustrating of people. ADD adults also now have a choice about counseling, rather than being dragged in by their parents.

The Basic Symptoms

The eight symptoms described before in ADD children can also appear, though often in modified forms, in adults. Many of the changes, of course, occur because school is replaced by a job, and the role of being a child is replaced by being a parent.

1. Inattention (Distractibility). Adults with ADD will often still find themselves having trouble concentrating on a number of things. They may find they have trouble staying on task when they are at work, with the result that they do not finish as much as they would like to. This kind of thing can also affect them around the house, where they can go from project to project without ever seeming to finish anything. Many ADD homemakers find that they can't seem to stay on top of household chores, and the day feels like one endless series of frustrations.

Inattentiveness also frustrates Attention Deficit adults in social situations, where they can have considerable difficulty focusing on conversations with others. Some of them find big parties or family get-togethers frustrating because so many conversations are going on at the same time, and they keep getting distracted from the one they are supposed to be paying attention to. This makes them run the risk of some embarrassment, if it becomes apparent to other people that they have lost the train of thought. They may also look to others as if they are bored, because they appear restless and do not always maintain eye contact.

2. Impulsivity. This symptom in adults may still be there, but it will be much more restrained than it is in ADD children. By the time they are adults, many of these people have been burned enough by past impulsive actions that they exercise more self-control. This may be especially true in social situations where they don't know the other people well. In fact, some ADD adults can be downright quiet when confronted with strangers! When they are comfortable with the other people or are with family, however, these adults often have a marked tendency to interrupt, blurt things out, and yell. Impulsivity can also appear when they are behind the wheel of a car, although it may be hard to say if ADD drivers are really worse than the average road maniac.

3. Difficulty delaying gratification. Impulsivity and difficulty with delay are similar problems. Impulsivity refers to action taken without thought and without waiting. Difficulty with delay is the sense of impatience and frustration stimulated by having to wait and think. In conversations ADD adults may have an awful time waiting to express their opinion about something. They may have trouble finding the patience for academic, "schoolish" like tasks such as balancing a check book, filing a tax return, or paying bills. Like the schoolchildren, they want to get these boring things over with as quickly as possible, and this often results in messy, unchecked work that can later come back to haunt them.

Some ADD adults also have serious problems managing money because they spend it too quickly. And since credit cards these days offer the promise of never having to wait for anything, they often find themselves pushing the credit limits on all their cards. Unfortunately, spending money can too easily be seen as an antidote to boredom. ADD adults often find that when they are inactive they are easily bored, and they can feel a sense of emptiness and melancholy that is hard for them to describe, but which they will do almost anything to avoid.

4. Emotional overarousal. In ADD children this symptom manifested itself primarily in the "hyper-silly" routine, especially in groups, and in ferocious tempers. In adults the hyper-silly behavior is much less common. Perhaps the adults have learned that it doesn't come across too well to other people, or perhaps they just don't feel like goofing around that often.

Temper is another story, however. ADD adults often continue to have tempers that are about as bad as those they had as children. Though these emotional outbursts may be restrained more in public, they will show themselves sometimes on the job with co-workers, or the problem may come across as a kind of persistent irritability. ADD people like this will often be described as moody by those that work with them. At home, unfortunately, the temper can be unleashed on spouse or children. Spouses often find that they have a very hard time asserting themselves with their ADD husband or wife, because so many of their interactions seem to involve anger. They begin to feel like they are always walking on eggs, and that the mood of the other person is quite unpredictable.

In addition, an ADD parent may continue to show a problem with low frustration tolerance when it comes to dealing with the kids. Since ADD tends to be hereditary, many of these kids are Attention Deficit themselves, so their behavior makes the problem doubly difficult.

People who are not Attention Deficit probably have no idea what kind of strain emotional overarousal regularly puts on the self-control of an ADD adult. These adults certainly do not ask that everything *feel* like a big deal, but it does. Non-ADD adults know what it is like to be more irritable at the end of a long day or after a few drinks, but this is an unusual experience for them. For ADD adults it is a regular, daily occurrence. It is almost as if the same event stimulates in them four times the amount of adrenalin that it does in someone else.

5. Hyperactivity. As they get older, most ADD people will tend to move around less. Gross-motor hyperactivity may be re-placed by a general kind of fidgetiness or restlessness, and some ADD adults are still described as not being able to sit still for very long. Others will continue to be hyperactive, but the hyperactivity will take a verbal form. Their speech may be rapid, nonstop, have a driven quality to it, and they may not be very good listeners.

6. Noncompliance. Certainly adults in general, as well as ADD adults, show less of a problem with following the rules. Part of this is simply due to the fact that they are in fewer situations where someone else is trying to tell them what to do, and as parents they are now trying to tell their kids what to do. Still, some studies indicate that as many as 25% of ADD adults may have a serious problem with antisocial behavior. Other retrospective studies of incarcerated adults suggest that large percentages of these people look as though they grew up with unrecognized Attention Deficit Disorder.

Many ADD adults function well enough in the workplace because they are their own boss. Others, however, may have quite a bit of difficulty with supervision, which tends to stir up some of the old "anti-parent" antagonisms that were experienced when they were kids (remember that some research showed that nine out of ten interactions between ADD kids and their parents were negative). Rules, therefore, may stimulate a kind of automatic opposition, and supervisors can be seen as stupid and irrational.

Because of their frequent inability to get their act together around the house, as well as their emotional lability, the spouses of ADD adults may sometimes feel like they have another kid to deal with rather than an equal partner. Trying to parent your own ADD spouse, however, is fraught with danger, because attempts at advice or correction are so often met with temper outbursts. So many non-ADD spouses simply keep their mouths shut, but inside feel considerable resentment toward their "partner."

7. Social problems. How one gets along with the rest of the human race is extremely important to anyone, and adults with ADD are no exception. Unfortunately, many of them feel isolated and rather lonely. It has been hard for them to keep long lasting relationships, and by the time they are adults some have simply quit trying. Inside they may often blame everyone else for their problems, but they also often have the feeling that they are the real source of their own troubles.

At home, their temper and bossiness can pose persistent difficulties to their spouse and the kids. At work, other people may find the ADD adult hard to be with due to their talkativeness, restlessness, tendency to complain, and general irritability. On the other hand, sometimes ADD adults are enjoyed for their lively personalities and their ability to get a party or something going, and this can help their social life considerably.

8. Disorganization. Many ADD adults have trouble juggling the different aspects of their lives. They can have trouble with dates, times and appointments, and—as it is with the ADD kids—their memory can be amazingly erratic. Their homes sometimes are monuments to their tendency to start and not finish things. The bathroom upstairs may have been torn up for the last six months, there are still paint cans on the floor of the kids' half-painted bedroom, and the car had to be parked outside all winter because the garage cleaning project never got done.

On the job, they have difficulty staying with a task, especially if they see it as boring and if it is solely up to them to keep going. It is also not unusual for them to feel like they are born procrastinators. Because they are easily bored, they tend to avoid tasks—like paper and pencil jobs—that they feel are uninteresting or obnoxious. They also tend to try to find the easiest or most interesting thing that they can do *right at the time*, but the problem with this way of operating is that their job of choice may not be what really needs to be done at that moment.

This has gotten some ADD adults into fairly sizeable trouble. The undone tasks build up. They feel more and more embarrassed about not doing them, but still can't bring themselves to face the unpleasantness. Then they are confronted by a supervisor who finally discovers the gap in their work, and they have no reasonable explanation for what happened.

For many ADD men and women, of course, life is pretty much OK. Most will be married, have jobs, and be self-supporting. A few who are bright, have reasonably decent social skills, and can use their extra energy to good advantage, can even be outstanding achievers. Even with these more fortunate ones, however, the residuals of Attention Deficit will continue to add some rough edges to their existence.

Note: For more information about ADD in adults, see the new video (available in March, 1994), *Adults with Attention Deficit Disorder*, by Thomas W. Phelan, Ph.D. See page 171.

16

Diagnosing ADD in Adults

How do ADD adults get into treatment? One would think that they would not especially care to see a mental health professional or physician, partly because many of them as kids felt they were dragged to every doctor in town. This may in fact be the case. Many people who work with ADD wonder where all the Attention Deficit adults are, since the data suggest there should be quite a few if 5% of children qualify and 60% of them don't outgrow their symptoms.

It is very common for adults to seek treatment for themselves after their ADD child has been successfully diagnosed and treated. In the course of their son or daughter's evaluation and therapy, they would have learned that ADD can be hereditary and that it is not outgrown. When discussing the developmental histories of their children, many adults can't help but reflect on their own childhoods, which are often remarkably similar to their kids. Involvement in support groups for parents often helps to reinforce the idea that residual ADD does exist, and parents may meet other parents whose histories are similar to their own. After enough of this enlightenment process, many men and women are convinced they are Attention Deficit themselves.

Spouses of ADD adults are often quite frustrated. This usually shows up in a frustrated wife, who knows she has an ADD kid but also feels convinced she has an ADD husband. Many of these women try to "encourage" their husbands to do something about their problem, but often the husbands are rather defensive and deny having anything wrong with them. It certainly is no help if one feels that seeking an evaluation for Attention Deficit is the emotional equivalent of eating crow.

Some adults have done a bit of their own diagnosing by trying out their child's stimulant medication on their own. This is not a recommended procedure, since it can backfire sometimes when the medication may be appropriate but the dosage is not. Others have such a good response that they bite the bullet and go into treatment, realizing they can't borrow meds from their kids for the rest of their lives.

After doing a fair amount of soul searching, many adults will come in stating that they are an ADD adult. Though most of these people are probably partially correct (there may be other diagnoses as well), the therapist needs to carefully check the available information and conduct an evaluation that is similar to what would be done with a child. In a few cases, some people may consider the diagnosis of ADD to be more benign than other diagnoses they may have had before, such as chemical dependency or even schizophrenia.

One of the most helpful considerations for the evaluator in this regard is chronicity. Though ADD without hyperactivity poses a problem here, to "qualify" as an ADD adult you must have been an ADD child. ADD does not just start up suddenly when you hit thirty-five. The diagnostician, therefore, must look at the presenting complaints and compare them to the eight symptoms. Then a careful developmental history must be done (which is not very easy when someone is already in their forties!), and, if possible, a lot of information collected.

The Evaluation Process

The diagnosis of adult ADD requires several steps. These include: 1) the self-reports of the adults themselves, 2) observation of their office behavior, 3) an interview with a spouse or other family member, and 4) the collection of certain other data.

    1. Self-reports. Many adults come into the office with their diagnosis in their hand. They may simply say something like, "I'm an ADD adult and I'd like to know what I can do about it." This self-assessment is often correct, but it still must be checked by the professional doing the evaluation, since there are a few people who are sometimes kind of shopping around for a more acceptable label for their chronic ills. These people sometimes aren't ADD at all, and may in fact be schizophrenic, alcohol or drug abusers, anxiety disorders, or sociopathic personalities. And there are, of course, many times when some of these other conditions, like drug abuse, exist along with Attention Deficit Disorder.

    What do ADD adults complain about if they come in? There are often three general problem areas that they are having difficulty with, and these involve depression, job concerns, and marital dissatisfaction. Both men and women can report the pervasive feelings of melancholy and dissatisfaction with life that accompany depression. Women are probably more honest about describing the sense of low self-esteem that usually goes along with this, while ADD males vacillate some between blaming everyone else for their troubles and being aware of their own shortcomings.

    Job concerns can involve the things mentioned earlier, and may be brought up more often by men than women. Difficulty concentrating, poor organizational skills, and difficulty getting along with others often give rise to a feeling that the person isn't progressing as quickly as he would like. For some ADD adults, these problems have been brought up in their periodic performance appraisals, which leave a residue of intense anger as well as nagging self-doubts.

    Marital problems are usually brought up by women. One reason for this may be that women in general are often looking for more out of a relationship than men are, so they may be the most frustrated with the state of the union and thus more likely to seek help for this. Many women are frustrated largely because of the ADD characteristics of their husband, but they find that it is very hard to persuade their mate to enter into counseling. If these fellows do ever show up, the would-be therapist may have quite a job on his hands trying to build some kind of useful therapeutic relationship.

With some ADD adults the complaints are less specific and sometimes presented in a rather confusing manner. Complaints of not being in a very good mood a lot of the time are common, and these may be mixed together with more vague hints about low self-esteem. A common theme that emerges often has to do with how aggravating other people are, and the list of culprits may seem endless, ranging from kids to wife to friends to government. Other less well defined complaints may have to do with not feeling well organized, difficulty persevering with different things, and a feeling of frequent memory loss or confusion.

2. Office behavior. Earlier it was mentioned that approximately 80% of ADD children will sit still in a doctor's office, probably because the situation is new and somewhat intimidating. Therefore, office behavioral observations are not always helpful in making the diagnosis for the little ones. The case is often different for the adults. Their behavior frequently shows a number of characteristics that can be observed and identified, and which do manifest the Attention Deficit symptoms.

Rapid speech is very common, and a steady flow of ideas may almost overwhelm the interviewer. The ideas are not very well organized, shifting from one to another, and the listener struggles at times to try to figure out what the point of a particular story is. The ADD adult may seem quite anxious, restless, driven, and sometimes presents an almost "haunted" look, as if they can't escape some dark cloud that follows them everywhere. Eye contact is often broken, and the person will sometimes appear as if they were lost in thought—pausing for a few seconds and kind of staring off into the room. One of the most common occurrences in interviews with ADD adults is their tendency to interrupt the interviewer. The symptom of difficulty delaying gratification seems to operate here. They suddenly get a good idea and simply can't wait to share it, so—irrespective of where you were in your sentence or thought—they just burst in with their idea. Many adults are aware of this and gently kid themselves about it from time to time, but that doesn't necessarily cut down the frequency.

The overall mood of the adult may alternate between sadness and irritation. So many things seem to irritate these people, and the emotional aftermath of this is sadness or brief depressive episodes. They are usually blaming all their woes on the behavior of other people, but once they trust a therapist, they can begin to get in touch with the real, deeper problems concerning what they think of themselves.

3. Interview with other family members. It is usually very important for the therapist or evaluator to talk with other people who know the possible ADD adult. For one thing, ADD adults—just like ADD kids—are not always good historians and they don't remember a lot of things that are important. In addition, they are not always objective and may have a distinct tendency to minimize certain aspects of their problems. While they might be quite candid, for example, when discussing their concentrational difficulties, they may omit and deemphasize a good deal when it comes to how they express their hostility at home with the family. Another reason for involving the spouse is that they will usually be quite helpful as (and if) treatment progresses.

Often the spouse is the person who will be interviewed, and they should be seen separately so they can talk freely. Many times the stress they feel is painfully obvious, and they welcome the opportunity to ventilate their own frustrations. They may describe their ADD mate as basically a moody individual, with the predominant moods being anger and depression. They also feel it is very difficult to talk to them and get anywhere, since everything appears to be taken as a criticism. Other common problems spouses may relate involve intolerance of the children, arbitrary and inconsistent discipline, and a host of unfinished projects around the house. Some people describe the guilt that they feel because they avoid their spouse or feel relieved when their partner is not around.

4. Collection of other data. With suspected ADD adults, the same information is helpful that is useful in diagnosing the kids. The only problem is that it is not as available. School records, including report cards, achievement tests, psychological testing, etc., are extremely helpful if they can be located. These pieces of information are also quite interesting to the person being evaluated, and they can help stimulate many important—as well as painful—memories.

Questionnaires, such as the Conners, also can be useful, but they were really designed for use with a population of children. Some evaluators, though, ask the client's mother—if she is available—to fill out the Conners as best she can as it would have applied when the person in question was about eight years old, or in approximately third grade. Sometimes the client himself can fill out the same questionnaire as best they can remember. This is certainly not a perfectly accurate procedure, but often the situations back in grammar school were so extremely difficult that useful information can be obtained.

It is also often useful to go through the seven prognostic indicators for ADD with the client, or with the client and his mother. Reviewing socio-economic status (when the client was a child), IQ, level of aggressiveness, hyperactivity, social skills, early detection, and family strength (or parental psychopathology) can be very enlightening.

If old psychological testing can be found, it can be very helpful, and again most clients will take quite an interest in reviewing it and having it explained to them. If psyc testing was never done, it might be a good idea to consider something like an adult IQ test and some achievement tests that have adult norms. Keep in mind here that if medication is to be considered later as a possible treatment alternative, the choice of a medication and its titration should probably be done before the testing is done, so as to get the most accurate results.

Another piece of information helpful with adults is the physical exam. This is probably more important here than with children, because the adults are much older, may have a greater range of possible physical problems, and may also have some difficulties with drug or alcohol misuse.

Diagnosis Shock

For the adults who are diagnosed as having Attention Deficit Disorder the discovery that they have a particular problem is something that has a number of positive as well as negative aspects. Many of these people almost feel that they are in a state of shock for a while as the "news" sinks in. The initial reaction is often something like "You mean it has a name!?" It's now like there is something inside me—a diagnosable disorder—that is not the same as my inner self.

On the positive side, this realization brings with it the idea that all this trouble may not have been my fault. It wasn't "just me" that was doing it. And all the people who have criticized me in the past didn't know the whole story. The ADD adult may also begin to feel that they are not alone. Other people, in fact, lots of other people, also suffer from the same problem. Sometimes comparing notes with these other adults can be a beneficial experience.

Also on the positive side is the feeling that perhaps something can be done about the problem. I don't have to be this way all the time. One of the most dramatic examples of this for many people is their first experience with medication. Some ADD men and women have experimented with their children's stimulant meds, and others have waited for their own prescriptions. For those who respond well to medication, the experience often feels like some kind of religious awakening. They can look at things and actually see them, paying attention to details that were previously unrecognized. They may suddenly be able to sit still during a conversation and really listen to what someone else is saying, without feeling the sense of restless urgency to either speak or leave. They can organize their daily activities and work more productively.

Many ADD adults will take antidepressant medication, either in addition to or instead of stimulants. Though its effects can take a week or two to kick in, a positive response to antidepressants can also be an enlightening experience. Some people will say that they never knew how depressed they were until they started feeling better. They had just taken that lousy feeling for granted for years.

On the negative side, the diagnosis of ADD can bring a sense of many wasted years. "If only I would have known I could have been saved a lot of trouble." This notion can also give rise to considerable anger toward those who didn't do anything about the problem in past years, especially one's parents. Even though this makes little sense—way back when there's no way anyone's parents could have known much about this kind of thing—the resentment can still be strong, especially when the ADD symptom of emotional overarousal adds its contribution.

Following the diagnosis, as a person learns more and more about Attention Deficit, other negatives can arise. Dramatic initial responses to medications, for example, can often generate hopes for a permanent cure or permanently altered state of being. Over a period of time, however, one realizes that ADD doesn't go away and that it is not curable. The effects of stimulant medications only last for a short period of time, and they usually can't be taken in the evening. Medications also involve expense, and for many people the idea of taking pills for the rest of their lives is not appealing. Some adults also find—as do some children—that the ADD symptom of disorganization makes it hard for them to stick to a regular medication regime.

For some men and women, Attention Deficit Disorder becomes a kind of obsession. It is almost as if diagnosis shock becomes a permanent condition itself. Their whole lives seem to revolve around ADD. All their thoughts and behavior are now interpreted as manifestations of Attention Deficit. The actions of other family members are often seen in the same light. The rest of the world may also be seen in a new light, and many other unsuspecting people will secretly be diagnosed. Comments such as, "My boss is so ADD I can't believe it!" or "There are too many ADD kids on this team for it to work," become more commonplace.

Those who become sort of obsessed with ADD also do a lot

of good. Many have made sizeable contributions to the development of support groups across the country. They have done a tremendous amount to increase awareness of ADD in the schools and the communities in which they live. In doing this they help themselves cope with their own problem and also help many children to avoid what they had to go through years ago.

17

Treatment of Adult ADD

Treatment of Attention Deficit in adults is often quite similar to what is involved in dealing with children (see Chapters 9-12). A "multimodal" approach is helpful, using several different strategies to attack the various aspects of the problem. This can include education about ADD, individual, marital, and family counseling, medication, and social skills training.

The Multimodal Approach

Adults need to be educated about ADD just as children do, but the adults are usually more interested in learning about the disorder and how it can affect them. Nowadays a good deal of educational material is available, and it is helpful for the ADD client to become acquainted with it and then to discuss it in counseling. Many people find it very interesting to learn about the basic symptoms of ADD and then to use this knowledge to shed light on their behavior.

This type of insight is often the necessary beginning of individual counseling. The therapist can assist the ADD individual in expressing their dismay and anger for having these symptoms, but also in taking responsibility for being the way they are and dealing with it. Accepting the fact of emotional overarousal in one's personality, for example, is not to be taken as license to abuse one's spouse or children. Individual counseling can also help a person come to some more realistic sense of self-esteem, an aspect of their existence which has usually taken quite a pounding over the years.

Marital counseling of some kind is also very often needed with ADD adults. A spouse's years of frustrations should be listened to (although not beaten to death), and something done to try to prevent the future from being as difficult as the past. Since the non-ADD spouse is often the underdog in the relationship, a therapist can also help the couple come up with a more democratic way of dealing with each other. The entire focus of counseling should not just be on Attention Deficit Disorder, however, since the ADD individual will also have legitimate gripes about their partner that need to be addressed.

Periodic family counseling can assist the children and parents in dealing with the usual problems that come with daily living, as well as those that are related to ADD. It is quite common, of course, for ADD parents to have ADD kids, and this can make for a very difficult combination around the house. The ADD adult will often find it helpful to become acquainted with some specific parenting strategies, such as counting, charting, or positive rein-forcement, rather than just shooting from the hip when problems come up.

Many of the same medications can be used with ADD adults that are used with ADD children. In the stimulant category, Ritalin and Dexedrine— and less often, Cylert—are commonly used and can be very helpful. The bodyweight formulas applicable to chil-dren in estimating therapeutic dosages (e.g., .5mg/kg for Ritalin), however, are not used with adults because of their lowered metabo-lism. Usually much less is needed. A 170 lb adult, for example, may do well with only 10 or 15 mgs of Ritalin per dose, or 15 mg of Dexedrine slow-release per day.

The tricyclic antidepressants, such as imipramine and

desipramine, as well as the "new generation" antidepressants, such as Prozac, Zoloft and Wellbutrin, are also useful in many situations, especially when depression poses an additional problem. Some people have suggested that the MAOI antidepressants can also be useful, but others worry that the necessary dietary restrictions required with these medications and the impulsivity and disorganization of ADD individuals can make for a dangerous combination.

Many adults find that the best medication regime for them involves using a stimulant and an antidepressant in combination. The reason for this is that the stimulants usually help with the core symptom—difficulty concentrating—and with temperament (restlessness, impulsivity, emotional overarousal, and impatience), but they are *short acting*. The antidepressants do not help usually with concentration, but they do help with temperament—and their effects can *last all day*. With both medications, therefore, an ADD adult may achieve a concentration benefit during the day, when it is most needed (at work), and may also maintain the temperamental "mellowing" effect during the evening (at home).

Although it seems to be used more with children, clonidine (Catapres) doesn't seem to be used very much in the treatment of ADD adults. Other psychotropic drugs have been used when other conditions exist along with Attention Deficit in adults, but there is not a lot of research on such therapy at the present. Even with the use of stimulants and antidepressants, medication therapy still involves a good deal of experimental trial and error. When it works, though, it is a critical part of the overall multimodal plan.

For adults, social skills training usually takes place in the context of individual counseling, rather than in a group setting. Therapists working with ADD often find it a refreshing change to work with an adult who wants to change his or her ways of relating to other people, rather than with an ADD child who is still blaming all their social ills on everyone else. Compared to children, ADD adults also have more of a chance to generalize their learning from the therapist's office to the real world, and many are delighted with thebenefits of their efforts. Medication can play a big role in effecting this social change for many individuals. Listening skills, for example, are often enhanced tremendously by stimulant medications when they are used in conjunction with counseling. Antidepressants can sometimes have a kind of calming effect that reduces the restlessness and fidgetiness that children, spouses, and co-workers find so irritating.

Issues and Questions

Although there is no doubt that ADD adults do exist, there are still plenty of questions that need to be answered about this often confusing subject. Here are several:

1. Where are all the ADD adults? If 5% of our school children qualify as Attention Deficit, and about 60% of them don't outgrow the problem, it is possible that 3% of the adult population could be experiencing significant ADD symptoms. Recently one magazine claimed that 20% of adults are ADD! Yet there definitely aren't this many men and women seeing therapists who are carrying a diagnosis of ADD. Undoubtedly, many don't come in for treatment, and others may be misdiagnosed.

2. What happens to the ADD girls when they become adults? As mentioned before, there may be a tendency for ADD girls in general to be less hyperactive than ADD boys. Therefore, they present fewer behavioral problems. For that very reason, though, they may not come to anyone's attention and may therefore go undiagnosed. As adults these women may still experience some of the concentration problems and disorganization that affected them when they were young, but they present a tricky diagnostic dilemma to any therapist. Their developmental history won't include things like hyperactivity, emotional overarousal, aggression, and other social problems. The person may also present herself as primarily depressed.

Some professionals believe, therefore, that ADD women seeking psychological treatment may be misdiagnosed. Of course, diagnosing depression and treating it with psychotherapy and antidepressant medication isn't such a bad idea, though the basic difficulty with concentration may still go untouched. Many ADD adults are going to qualify for more than one kind of diagnosis, and the second one may very well be depression.

A bigger problem may occur when many of these women are seen as having manic-depressive illness (also known as bipolar disorder). Because of their moodiness and melancholy, some mental health professionals see these adults as bipolar "rapid cyclers." This is supposed to mean that the manic and depressed cycles of that disorder come more often. ADD moodiness, however, is a daily or hourly occurrence, and is not at all the same as rapid cycling. If ADD women, therefore, are diagnosed as bipolar disorder and are treated with lithium and possibly major tranquilizers (such as Mellaril), their problems are not going to be effectively addressed.

3. How do you counsel or treat ADD adults effectively? With Attention Deficit Disorder, the client's problems often can directly interfere with their treatment compliance and therefore with the effectiveness of therapy. Because of their forgetfulness, for example, missing appointments or coming to the office on the wrong day or at the wrong time are not unusual. Medication use can sometimes be rather erratic. This can lessen the effectiveness of stimulants such as Dexedrine and Ritalin, but it can destroy any benefit from the antidepressants, which need to be taken regularly every day.

4. How long can a therapist deal with large numbers of ADD clients? Dealing with ADD children is quite taxing, partly because of the large cast of characters that must come along for the ride for treatment to be effective. Parents, teachers, pediatricians, siblings, special education personnel, and others often have to be involved. It is not always much different when dealing with an ADD adult; other people can often help a lot, but this requires more time coordinating everyone on the team and a lot more phone calls. In addition, the family members of ADD people—children and adults— many times have their own psychological problems (e.g., depression, alcoholism, hysteria, anxiety) that complicate the picture and make them harder to work with. It sometimes feels as though the whole scenario is tailor made to produce rapid therapist burnout.

5. Finally, what about insurance coverage for treatment? With all the people—mostly kids—who have been diagnosed so far as ADD, insurance companies are becoming more reluctant to provide coverage, citing reasons such as preexisting condition rules or claiming that ADD is not a medical diagnosis. Adult ADD is also not yet included in the diagnostic manual. Though comorbidity may provide some help here (something else may be legitimately diagnosed for coverage to kick in), this problem, plus the difficulties involved in evaluating adult ADD in the first place, make for a confusing situation.

In spite of these difficulties, the fact that Attention Deficit is finally being recognized in adults may mean a much more productive future for millions of men and women.

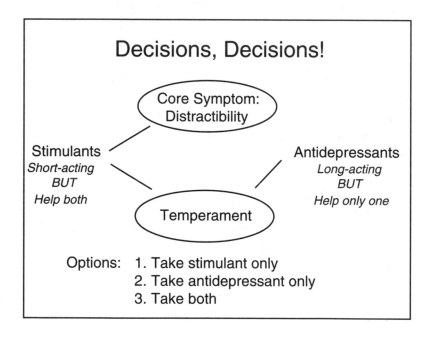

For More Information...

General:

- Barkley, Russell. *Attention Deficit Hyperactivity Disorders: a Handbook for Diagnosis and Treatment.* New York: Guilford Press, 1990.
- Ingersoll, Barbara. *Your Hyperactive Child.* Doubleday, 1988.
- Phelan, Thomas W. *All About Attention Deficit Disorder* (Video 1990, Book 1994). Child Management, Inc. (800) 442-4453.

School Related:

- Parker, Harvey C. *The ADD Hyperactivity Handbook for Schools.* Impact Publications, Plantation, FL, 1992. (305) 792-8944
- *The CH.A.D.D. Educators Manual,* 1992. Available from Caset Associates, (800) 545-5583.

Medication:

- Copeland, Edna. *Medications for Attention Disorders and Related Medical Problems.* 3 C's of Childhood, 1991.
- *Journal of Child and Adolescent Psychopharmacology.* New York: Mary Ann Liebert, Inc.
- Phelan, Thomas W., & Bloomberg, Jonathan. *Medication for Attention Deficit Disorder.* (Video). Child Management, Inc., 1994. (800) 442-4453.

Adult ADD:

- Phelan, Thomas W. *Adults with Attention Deficit Disorder.* (Video). Child Management, Inc., 1994. (800) 442-4453.
- Weiss, Lynn. *Attention Deficit Disorder in Adults.* Taylor Publishing, 1992.

Managing ADD Children:

- Phelan, Thomas W. *1-2-3 Magic: Training Your Preschoolers and Preteens to Do What You Want* (Book, Video). Child Management, Inc., 1991. (800) 442-4453.
- Phelan, Thomas W. *Surviving Your Adolescents: How to Manage and Let Go OF Your 13 to 18 Year Olds.* (Book) Child Management, Inc., 1993. (800) 442-4453.

For the Kids:

- Dixon, E. and Nadeau, K. *Learning to Slow Down and Pay Attention.* Chesapeake Psychological Services, 1991.
- Gehret, Jeanne. *I'm Somebody Too.* Verbal Images Press, 1992.
- Gordon, Michael. *Jumpin' Johnny: Get Back to Work.* GSI Publications, 1991.
- Moss, Deborah. *Shelly the Hyperactive Turtle.* Woodbine House, 1989.
- Parker, Roberta N. and Parker, Harvey C. *Making the Grade: an Adolescent's Struggle with Attention Deficit Disorder*. Impact Publications, 1992.
- Quinn, P.O. and Stern, J. *Putting on the Brakes.* Magination Press, 1991.

Newsletters:

- *CH.A.D.D.ER.* Semi-annual publication of CH.A.D.D. (305) 587-3700.
- *CHALLENGE*. Publication of the National Attention Deficit Disorder Association. (508) 462-0495.

Catalog of ADD books, audios, and videos:

- **A.D.D. WareHouse** (800) 233-9273 or (305) 792-8944.